KEY IDEAS

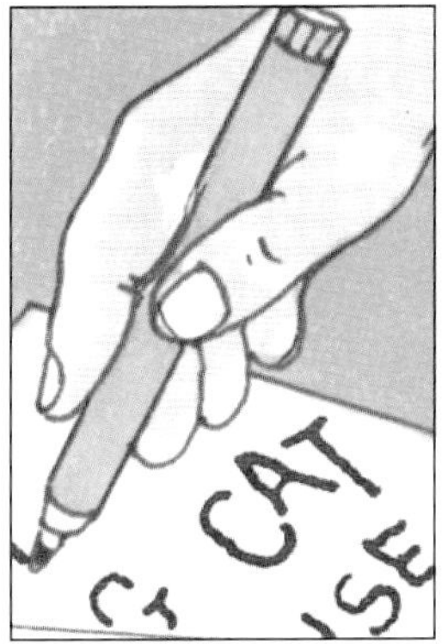

Writing

Chris Webster

Acknowledgements

First published in 1997 by Folens Limited, Dunstable and Dublin
Folens Limited
Albert House
Apex Business Centre
Boscombe Road
Dunstable LU5 4RL
England

The author and publisher thank the following:
Charlotte Whitehouse and Jonathan Ball for their illustrations.
The children and staff of the following schools for allowing us to photograph their work: St Anne's RC, St Helens; St Marie's RC, Kirkby; Moss Pits Jnr, Liverpool; Cronton CE, Cronton, Merseyside; Hobbs Hill Wood Jnr, Hemel Hempstead.
The teachers and staff of the following Service Children's Schools (North-West Europe): Andrew Humphrey, Wildenrath; Blankenhagen, Gütsersloh; Bückeburg; Cheshire, Brüggen; Haig, Gütersloh; Krefeld; Montgomery, Hohne; Oxford, Münster; St Andrew's, Rheindahlen; Sir John Mogg, Detmold; and Wellington, Osnabrück.

Editor Hayley Willer
Layout artist Suzanne Ward
Photographs The photograph on page 41 (top) is reproduced courtesy of Georgina Stein.
Illustrations Peter Fox
Cover image Frances Mackay
Cover photograph Bill Osborn
Series design Andy Bailey
Cover design Kim Ashby and DFM

British Library Cataloguing in Publication Data. A catalogue record for this book is available from the British Library.

Printed in Great Britain by Jarrold Book Printing, Thetford, Norfolk.

ISBN 1 85276194-6

Contents

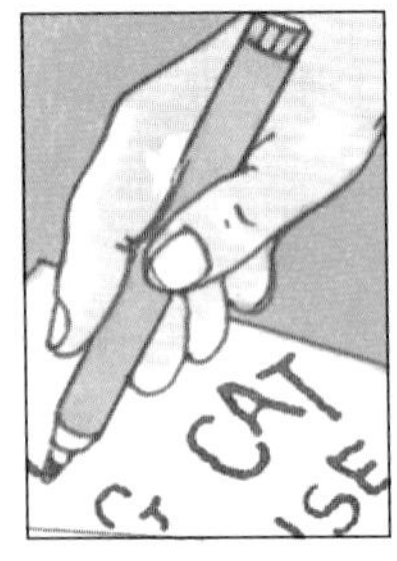

Introduction

Children should be given opportunities to write for a wide variety of purposes. It is important they understand that, amongst other things, writing is a tool for planning and organising as well as for communication.

Often in schools today, children do much of their writing when working in subject areas other than English. This writing is for a whole range of purposes, from writing a time line of events for a history project to recording the results of a science experiment.

This book aims to provide examples of the different types of writing that children can undertake and enjoy. It is organised into areas that are topical and relevant to children's lives today. Types of writing range from letter-writing, in which children should be taught the formalities of presentation and effective communication, to the writing of campaigns in which children should develop the skills of interviewing, reporting and writing to persuade.

Each of the ten chapters begins with a statement of aims and an introduction. These are followed by advice on preparation, including the resources required, and the kinds of preparatory tasks children could usefully undertake. A range of specific activities is then described in words and photographs. This includes, where appropriate, an IT-based activity. Each section ends with suggestions for follow-up activities.

Above all, the ten chapters are intended to be more than a collection of specific lesson ideas. Taken together, they represent an approach to the teaching of writing which can be applied across the whole curriculum in a way that will not only lead to a wider range and higher quality of written work but also enhance the quality of learning in the specific subject areas. This development can be monitored through use of the photocopiable assessment sheets at the back of this book.

To help the children get the most from their writing, a supportive context needs to be provided. There are three main aspects to this: setting up writing areas, providing displays and helping children to understand the writing process. The latter point involves understanding the importance of drafting and redrafting, awareness of intended audience and the advantages of evaluating completed work.

A celebratory display on the bee.

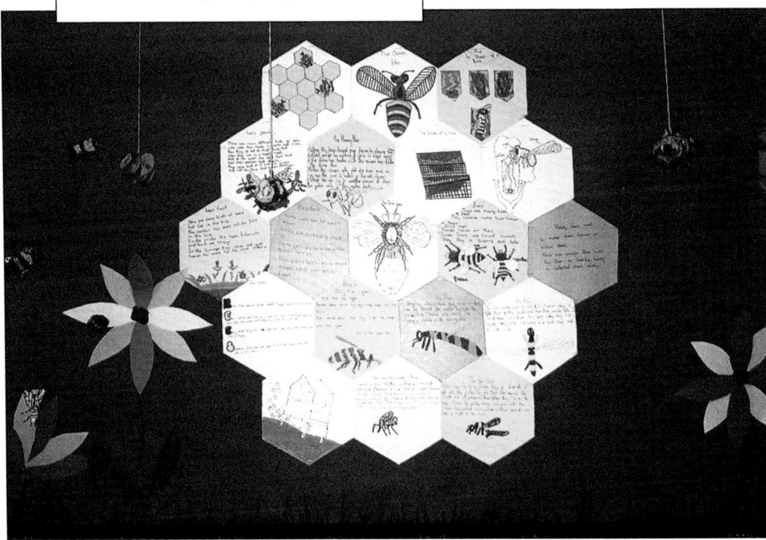

Writing areas

A writing area is a well-equipped work-station for those who wish to write during a multi-activity lesson. Writing areas need to be attractively laid out and should include some or all of the following:

- a range of paper, pens and pencils
- dictionaries, thesauruses, word banks, spell checkers
- starter ideas and prompts.

Displays

Displays fall into two broad categories.

- Instructional displays provide support for children as they work – they are a constant reminder of important writing skills.
- Celebratory displays, of which there are many examples throughout this book, consist of children's completed work.

The writing process

The drafting process is one of the most important things that we can teach children, because it is in the shaping and polishing of work that real learning takes place.

Children should be encouraged to write down some ideas, however sketchy, in a first draft. An example of writing at this stage can be seen in the photograph on the right. The work should then be redrafted. This stage provides excellent teaching opportunities. For example, a child can be helped to develop description, or improve spelling and punctuation. The final copy should be neatly presented, as in the photograph below. An illegible communication is, of course, pointless, and the piece of work should be clearly structured, correctly punctuated and in neat handwriting.

The final copy is neatly presented.

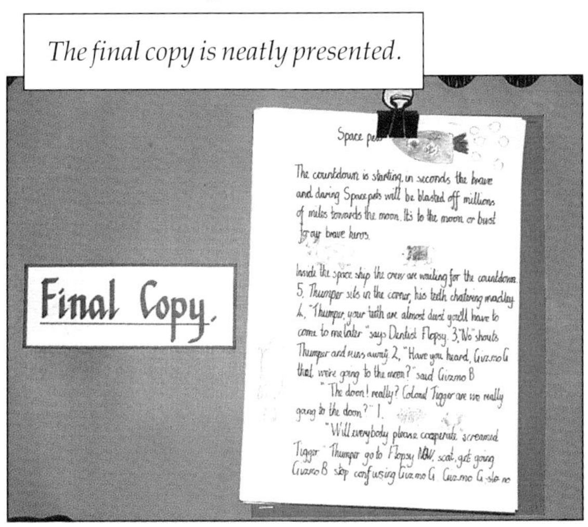

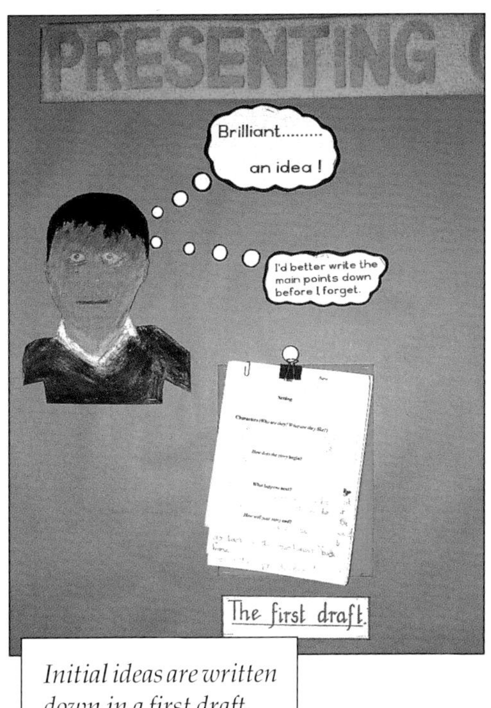

Initial ideas are written down in a first draft.

Audience and purpose

Children write best when they know the audience and purpose for their writing. This provides motivation, as well as a clearer sense of what vocabulary and style is appropriate. It also provides a genuine need for neat presentation and accuracy.

Evaluation

It is always a valuable exercise, when a project is completed, to ask the children to look back at what they have done and evaluate its usefulness. Could they have presented something more attractively? Did they include as much information as they could? Did they refer to reference books and dictionaries while writing? The results of such evaluations will help them to develop skills of a higher order and to present better quality work in the future.

Food

Planning a party

The oldest examples of writing are organisational: lists of stores, taxes, arms and so on. Writing for organisational purposes is just as important today, and one way for the children to explore it is by planning a party.

Aims

To develop the skills of:

- planning
- writing notes and lists
- designing the layout of written information.

Party

Karina

People to invite	Food	Games
Jessica	Cakes	Presents
Jennifer	Jelly	Pass the parcel
Tracey	Ice cream	Snakes and Ladders
Mirrika	Jam tarts	Simon Says
Lisa	buns	Musical st
Lauren	Chicken	dominoes
Edward	burger	Chicken
Warren	drinks	Limbo
Christie	birthday cakes	
Zoe	meat	

Planning a party gives the children a real reason to practise writing lists.

1 Preparation

- Planning a party can be done as a group exercise. The run-up to Christmas is a good time for these activities, as the children could be planning a real class party. They should be encouraged to:
  - discuss with an adult how many people will be invited, how long the party will last and where it will take place
  - list the people to invite
  - list the activities to take place together with the duration of each
  - list the food that is needed and the food that needs to be bought
  - list non-food items that need to be bought, such as candles and hats.

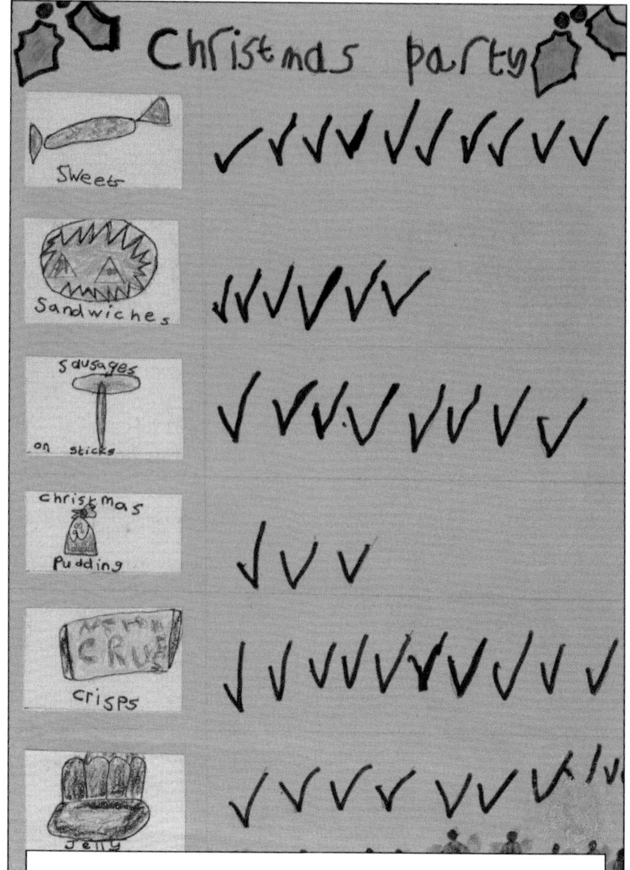

This chart was used to determine which food would be the most popular at the party and so helped with the decisions as to what and how much to buy.

Food

2 Design and write

- When the guest lists and style of party food have been decided, provide the children with paper and coloured pens – and a computer if you have one – so that they can make the invitations, menus and place cards.

The children could make a colourful menu to place in the centre of the table. This menu was produced in the context of a history topic.

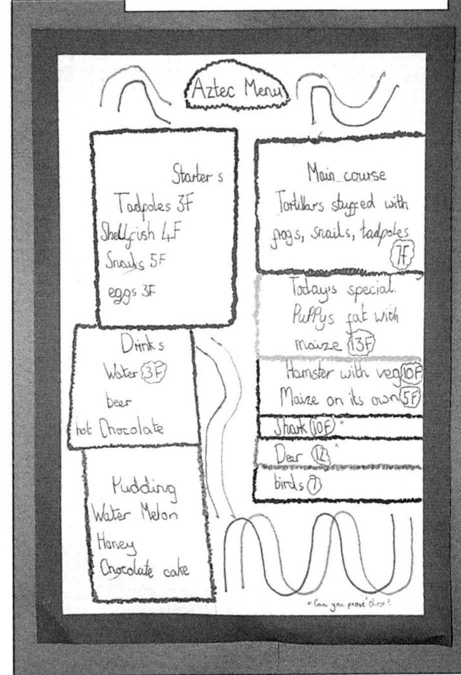

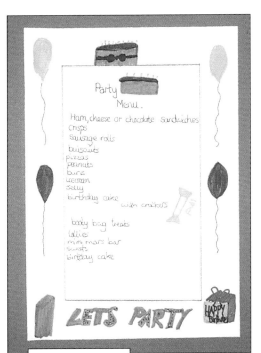

This menu was produced for a birthday party.

3 Information technology

- Most desktop publishing programs come with a range of clipart (pictures), including party clipart. This can be used to produce invitations on the computer.

INVITATION

PARTY

to Jenny Wilson

I am having a party at 4.00pm
on Monday 4th June.
Can you come?

I can/I cannot come.............................

This invitation was produced on a computer using clipart.

Extension activity

- The children could write thank-you letters to those who gave presents and helped with the organisation. They could use a computer 'mail merge' facility to do this.

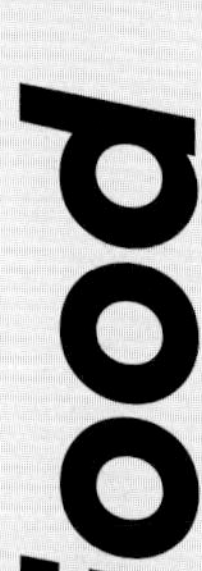

Recipes

Recipes are a good example of instructional writing. They must be clear, accurate and easy to follow. Any weakness in the writing will show up when the food is eaten!

Aim

To develop the skill of:

- writing precise and detailed instructions.

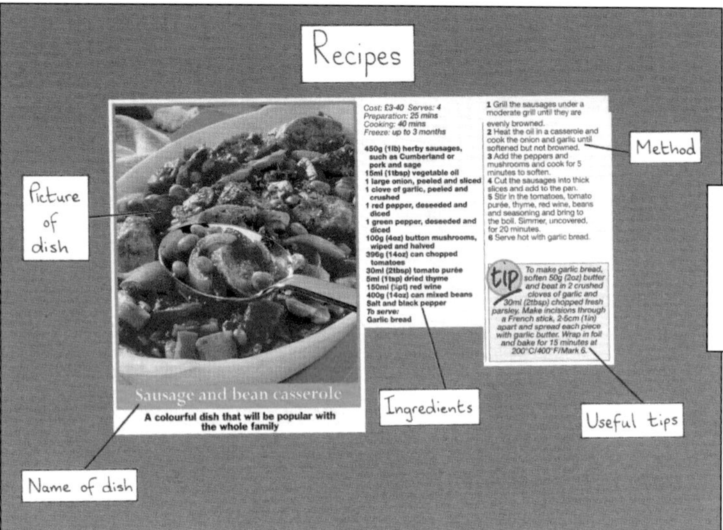

Looking at published recipes from cookery books and magazines helped the children to become familiar with the style of writing used.

1 Preparation

- Let the children study some examples of recipes. Help them to see that each recipe contains:
  - a list of ingredients, showing the amounts needed (older recipes and American recipes use measurements other than metric ones)
  - step-by-step instructions
  - illustrations.
- Make sure that the children understand that instructions are written in the second person (for example, 'you will need three eggs'). They may find it difficult not to describe what 'I' or 'we' did.

2 Write a recipe

- The children could think of a dish with which they are familiar and write a recipe for it. For instance:
  - cheese on toast
  - scrambled eggs on toast
  - cheeseburger
  - pizza.

The children made a list of the recipes that they felt they could write for a class recipe book.

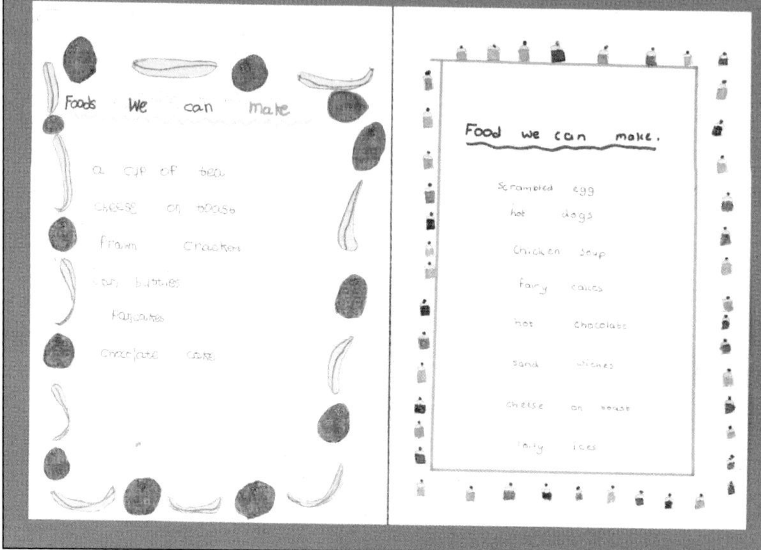

Food

3 Class recipe book

- The whole class could collaborate to produce a class recipe book.
- Begin with discussion and negotiation to avoid duplicating the recipes. Let the children work individually or in pairs, using a standard size of paper such as A3.
- They should be advised to place the title of their recipe and the list of ingredients in the same place on each sheet, but be free to set out the instructions in any way that they like.
- Encourage simple but imaginative approaches to food preparation.

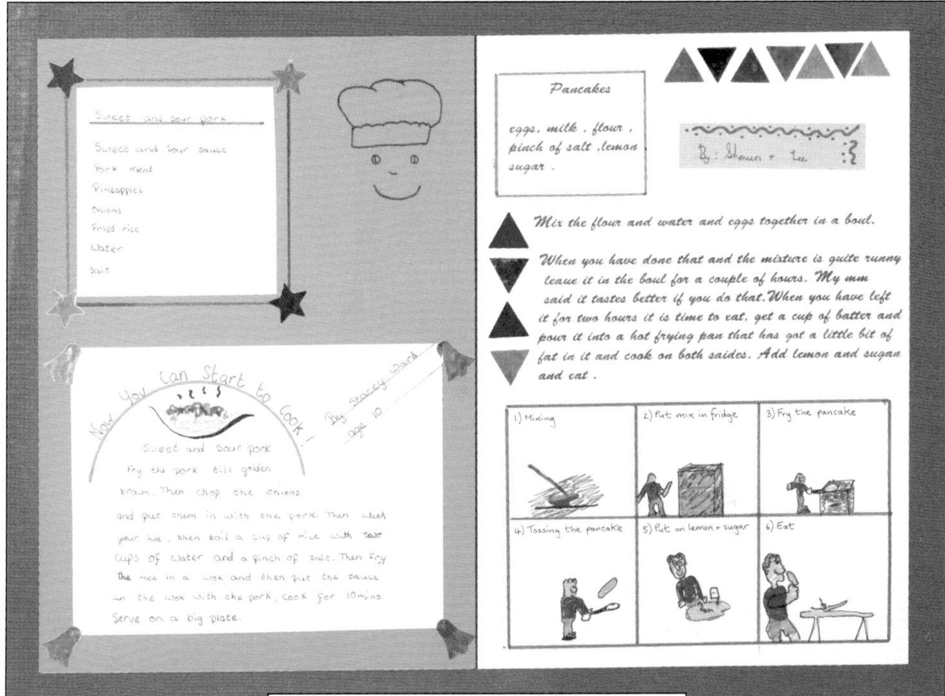

Once the recipes were finished they were pasted into a class recipe book.

CLASS 4
RECIPE BOOK

Some of the children designed a cover for the class book.

4 Information technology

- One group could enter the recipes into a database. *DataPower* by Iota Software is a good example of a simple modern database for Acorn computers. *Cardbox* is a similar program for PCs which is included with Windows software.

Extension activities

- A selection of the recipes could be made – perhaps for a class party. The children preparing the food should not be the same group that wrote the recipe.
- The children could discuss which aspects made the recipes most helpful.

Healthy eating

An important part of health education is learning about healthy eating. It is good for the children to carry out their own research on this subject, for this equips them to make independent decisions about food rather than be influenced by fashions in diet and advertising.

Aims

To develop skills of:
- research
- writing to inform
- writing to persuade.

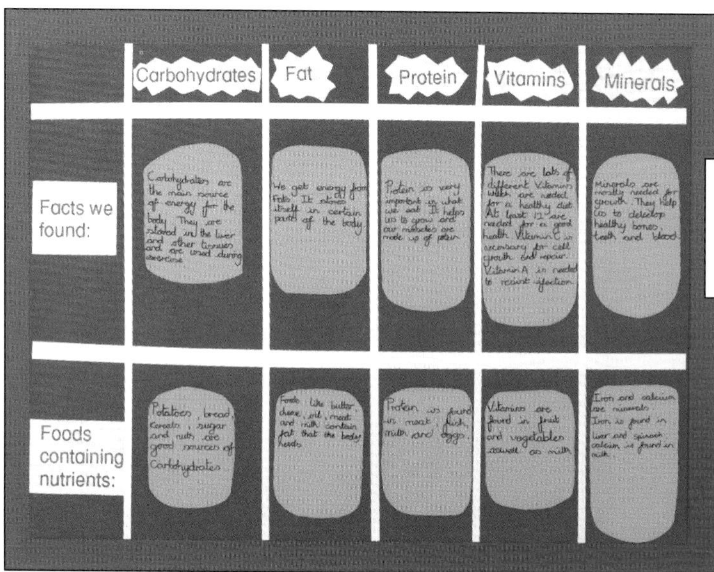

The children researched facts about food and produced a chart.

1 Preparation

- Help the children to carry out thorough research into the scientific facts about protein, carbohydrates, fat, vitamins and calories. They could research:
  - how much of each the body needs
  - how much of each is found in common foods.
- They could find out about food hygiene:
  - washing fruit and vegetables
  - preserving food safely
  - cleaning teeth.

2 Persuading others

- Encourage the children to use their findings to educate others about healthy eating. They could present their message in a variety of forms, including:
  - charts
  - leaflets
  - posters
  - guide books
  - stories and poems.

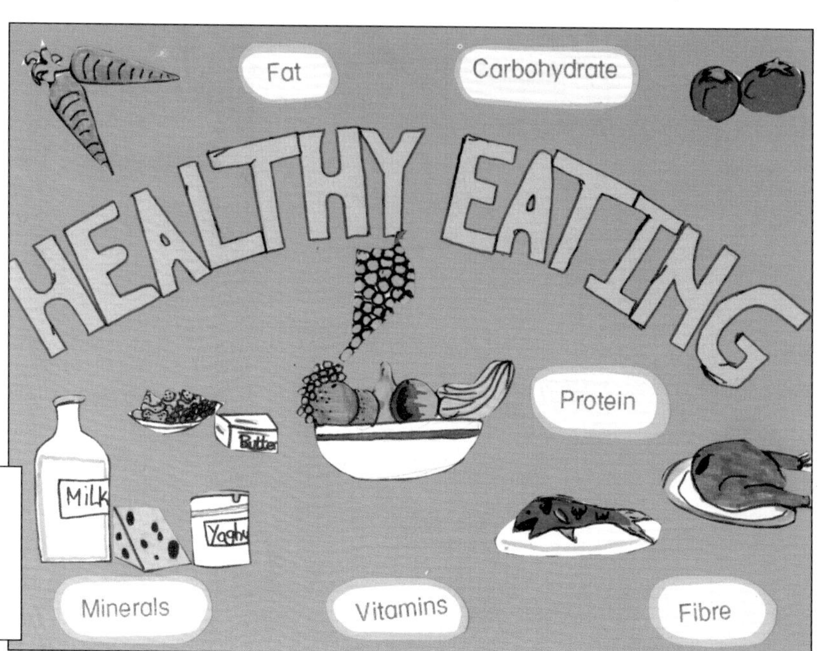

A poster conveys information effectively and immediately. The children made a poster advertising good foods.

3 Eating diary

- The children could keep an eating diary for a week.
- They should then consider what they have eaten and, with the help of reference books, decide whether it was a healthy diet.
- Using the conclusions drawn, they could plan a healthy diet for the following week.

Some of the children kept an eating diary for a week and compared them before deciding who had a healthy diet.

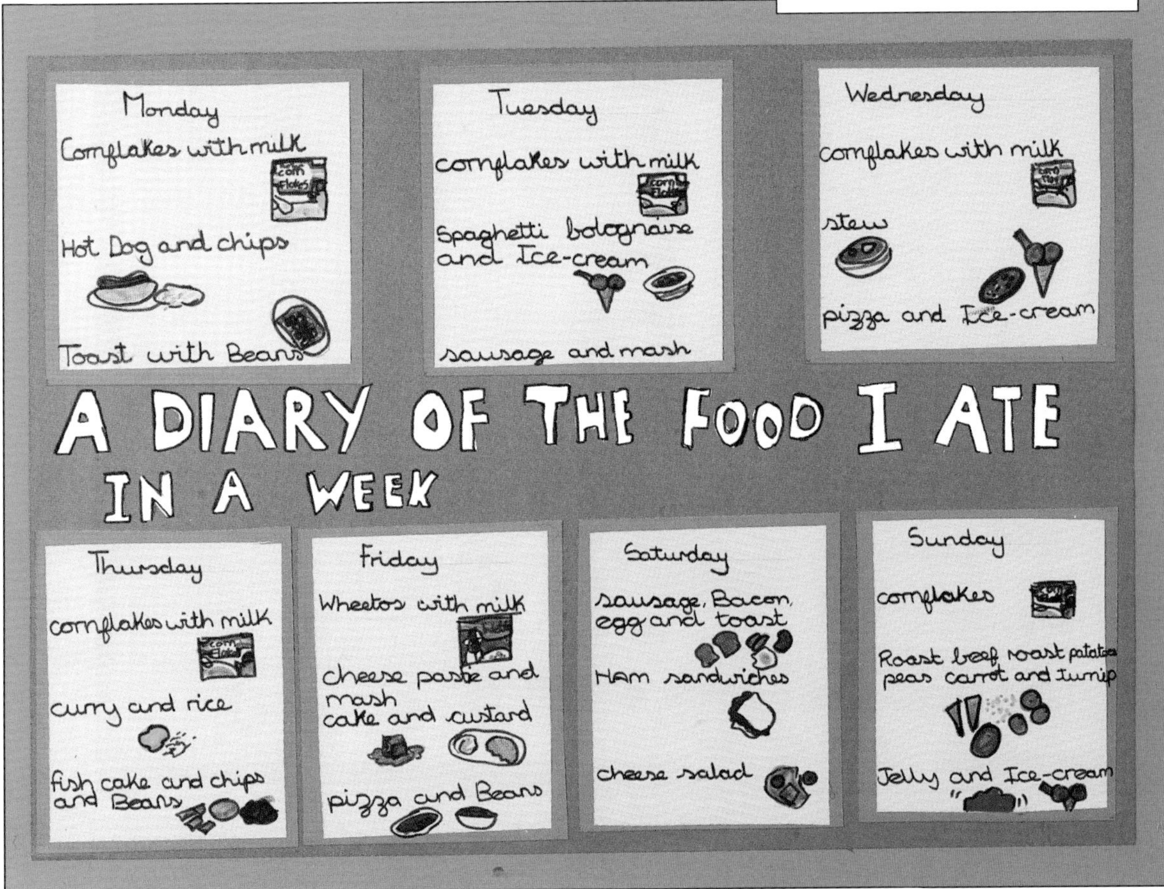

4 Information technology

- Programs are available that will analyse a diet and suggest improvements. *Fruit* and *Veg* by Semerc are two examples of such programs. They include calorific and nutritional values of a whole range of fruit and vegetables and allow the user to plan a healthy diet.
- The children could plan a diet and use one of these programs to analyse it.

Extension activity

- The children could use the information gained from their research as the basis of a healthy eating campaign for the school.

The school

The best place to begin a study of the environment is in the immediate locality. The school is a good place to start, since it consists of both indoor and outdoor environments which have to serve a wide variety of needs.

Aims

To develop skills of:

- collecting and recording evidence about places and geographical issues
- analysing evidence and communicating findings.

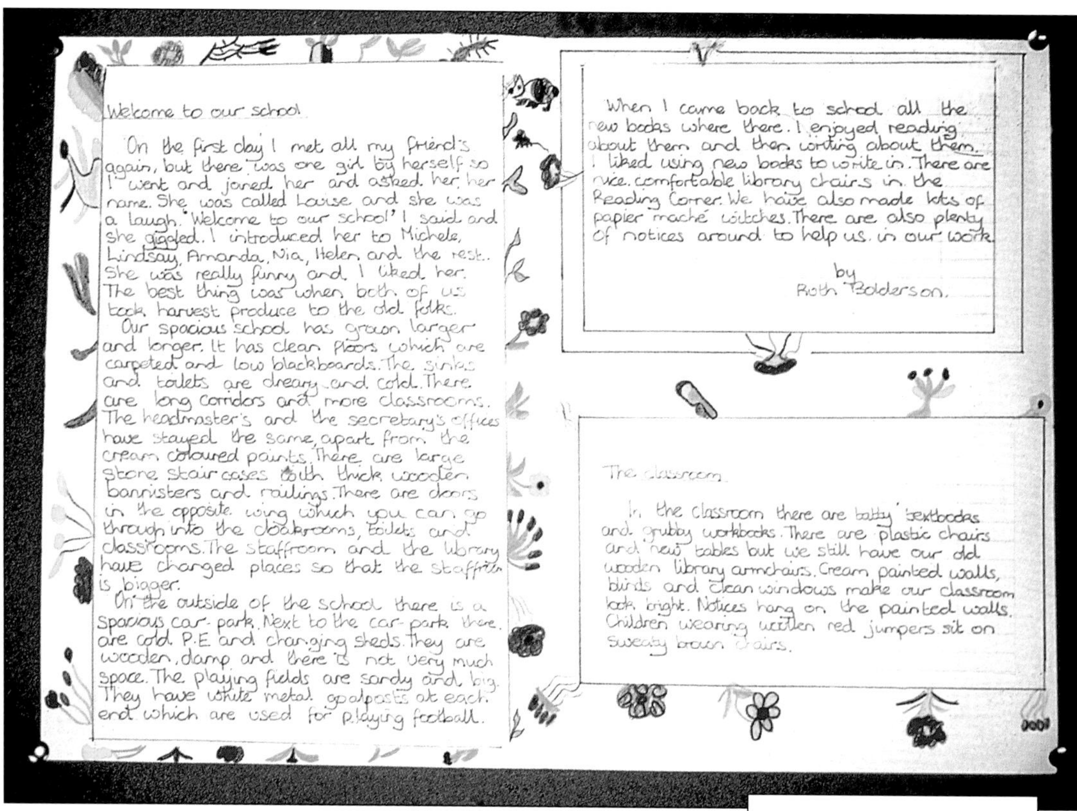

Welcome to our school.

On the first day I met all my friend's again, but there was one girl by herself so I went and joined her and asked her her name. She was called Louise and she was a laugh. 'Welcome to our school' I said and she giggled. I introduced her to Michele, Lindsay, Amanda, Nia, Helen and the rest. She was really funny and I liked her. The best thing was when both of us took harvest produce to the old folks.

Our spacious school has grown larger and larger. It has clean floors which are carpeted and low blackboards. The sinks and toilets are dreary and cold. There are long corridors and more classrooms. The headmaster's and the secretary's offices have stayed the same, apart from the cream coloured paints. There are large stone staircases with thick wooden bannisters and railings. There are doors in the opposite wing which you can go through into the cloakrooms, toilets and classrooms. The staffroom and the library have changed places so that the staffroom is bigger.

On the outside of the school there is a spacious car park. Next to the car park there are cold P.E. and changing sheds. They are wooden, damp and there is not very much space. The playing fields are sandy and big. They have white metal goalposts at each end which are used for playing football.

When I came back to school all the new books where there. I enjoyed reading about them and then writing about them. I liked using new books to write in. There are nice comfortable library chairs in the Reading Corner. We have also made lots of papier maché witches. There are also plenty of notices around to help us in our work.

by

Ruth Bolderson.

The classroom.

In the classroom there are tatty textbooks and grubby workbooks. There are plastic chairs and new tables but we still have our old wooden library armchairs. Cream painted walls, blinds and clean windows make our classroom look bright. Notices hang on the painted walls. Children wearing woollen red jumpers sit on sweaty brown chairs.

One child described her school environment.

1 Preparation

- Discuss with the children possible improvements to the school buildings and grounds. They could study this environment in small groups, making detailed notes as they go. Each group could focus on a different aspect, such as:
  - brightening up corridors
  - tidying and organising the classroom
  - constructing a pond or garden
  - conducting a litter search
  - improving play areas
  - improving safety.

2 An improvement plan

- After their school investigations, each group should discuss what they have seen, agree what their recommendations will be and then:
  - list the materials needed
  - estimate the cost
  - draw up plans.
- The groups could pool their recommendations in order to make an improvement plan for the whole school. This could be presented to the head teacher, with the possibility of actually carrying out some of the improvements.

3 Presenting the recommendations

- The children's recommendations for improvement should be communicated in an attractive and effective way.

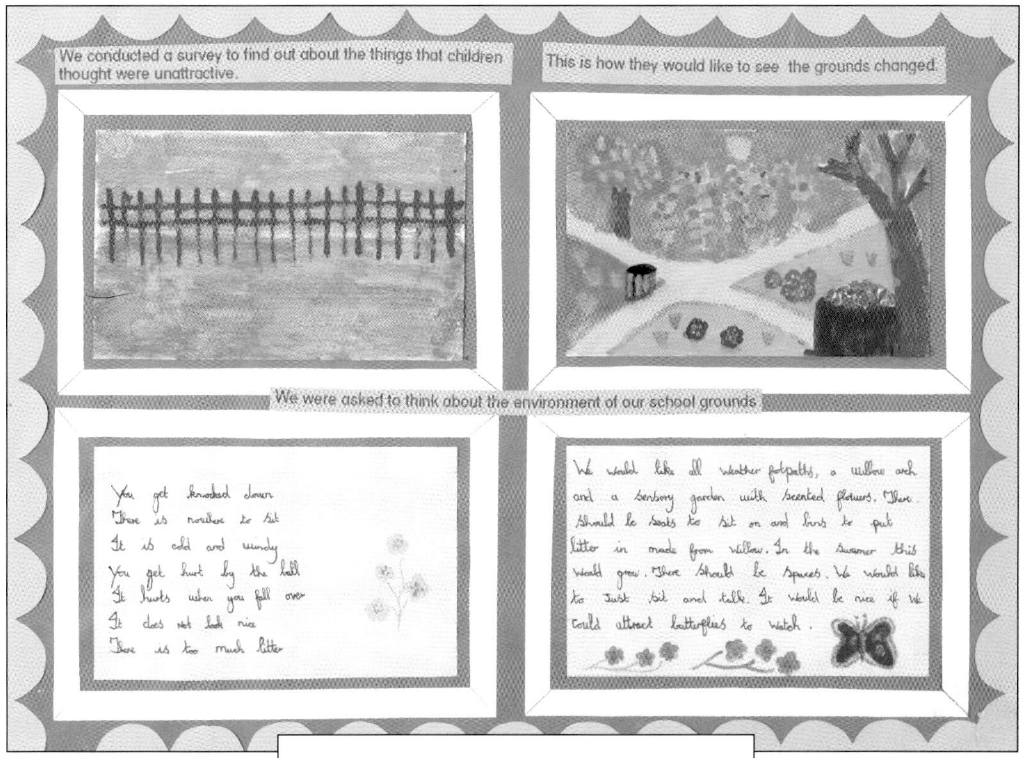

The children looked at the school grounds and suggested how to improve them.

4 Other suggestions

- To encourage pride in the school, the children could put forward designs for a new badge or item of uniform, such as a sweatshirt or baseball cap.

One child designed a school baseball cap.

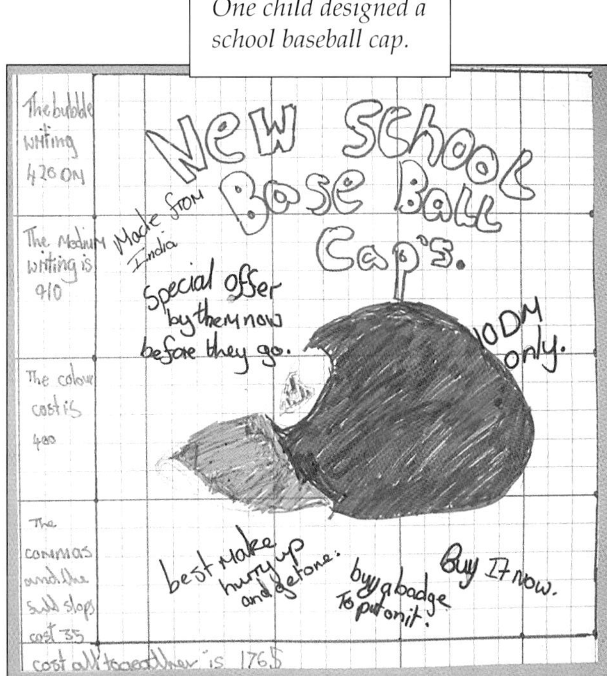

Extension activity

- The children could compare their own school environment with one in a contrasting locality. This could include communicating with the other school by sending written messages through a fax machine.

Environments

The locality

An exploration of the wider local environment follows naturally from a study of the school and provides an ideal focus for investigative work and the presentation of findings.

Aims
To develop skills of:
- collecting and recording evidence
- communicating the findings in a variety of forms.

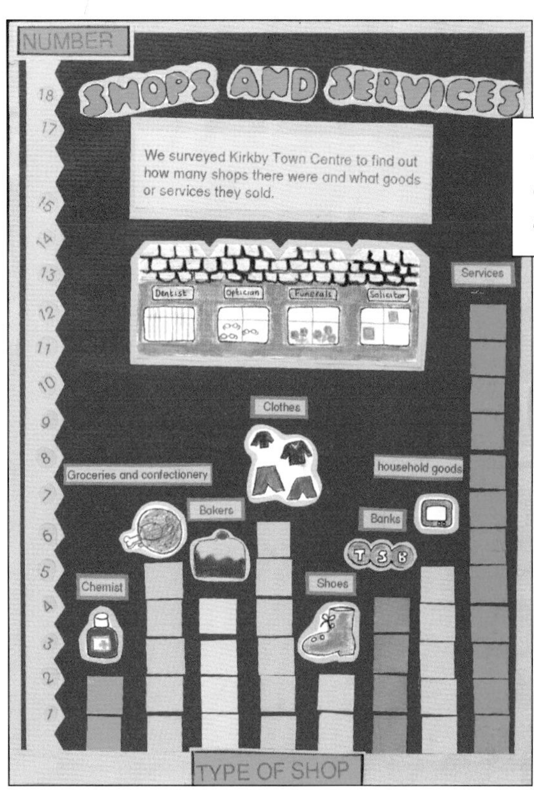

One group of children surveyed shops in the area.

1 Preparation

- The children should find out as much as they can about the immediate locality. They could go on a 'field trip', make notes when they go out with their parents and collect information such as maps, aerial photographs and postcards. Their research could cover:
  - housing (different types)
  - high street shops and any 'out of town' shops such as supermarkets
  - communications, such as roads and railways
  - services, such as schools, medical centres, banks, garages, libraries and post offices
  - interesting old buildings
  - places of worship, such as churches
  - local industries
  - any special features, such as in a seaside town.

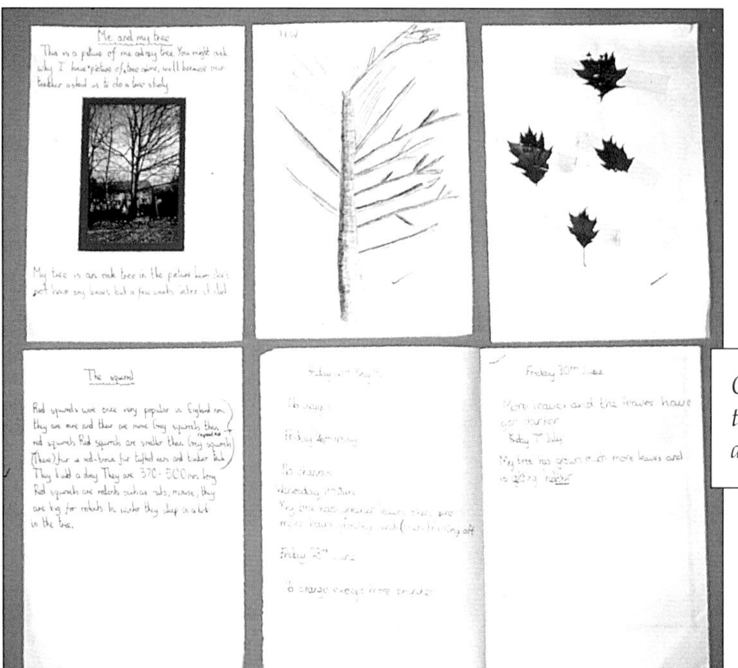

One girl decided to investigate the very small environment of a favourite tree.

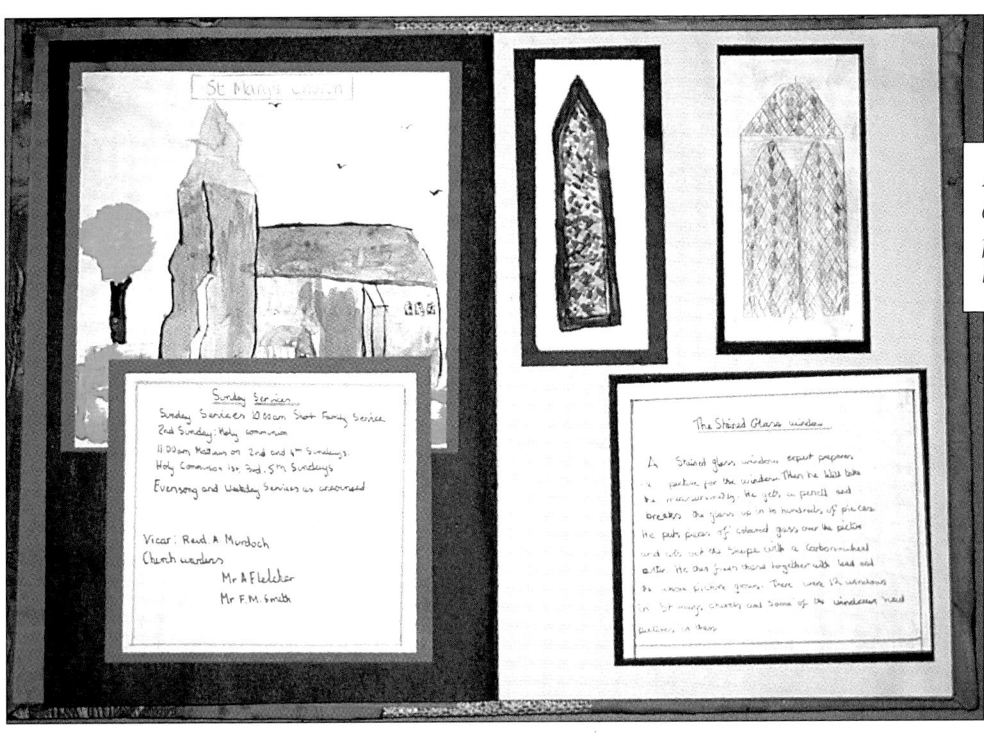

A detailed study of one particular place in the locality.

2 Design

- The children could use the information they have collected to design publicity material about their town.

They should start by making clear decisions about purpose and audience. For example, will the publicity materials:

– provide information for new residents
– advertise the town as a place to visit
– advertise the town to attract new business?

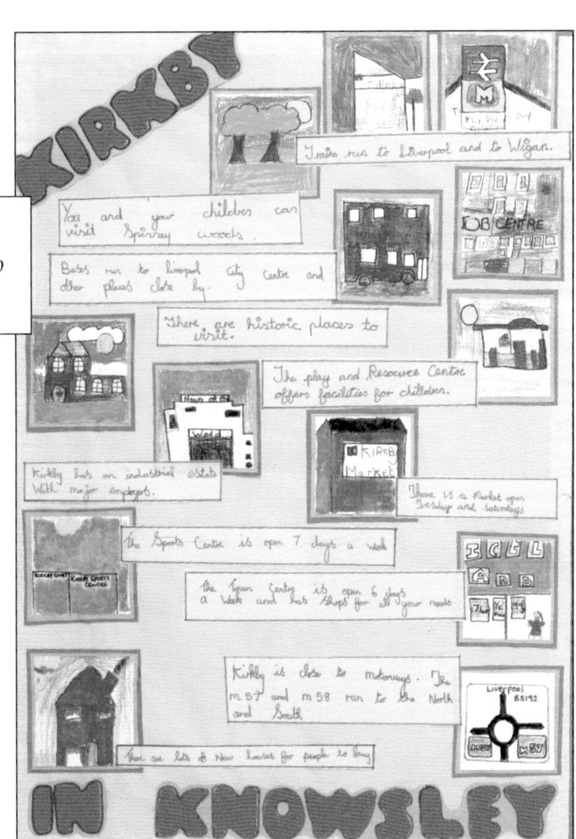

An advertisement explaining the attractions of the town to people who are looking for somewhere to live.

3 Information technology

- The children could present their information in a database which might be placed in a public library. A database such as *Genesis* or *Hypercard* will allow scanned photographs and maps to be displayed. Categories could include:
  – where to shop
  – places of interest.

Environmental issues

The children can be helped to understand that the quality of our environment depends on the choices we make as a society. Those choices are influenced by the ability of different interest groups to persuade others to think as they do.

Aim

To develop the skill of:

- writing to persuade.

As part of a litter survey, some children investigated different types of waste.

1 Preparation

- Divide the class into groups and ask each group to agree upon an environmental issue to research. The issues that arise may include:
  - recycling
  - conservation areas
  - river pollution
  - problems of litter
  - the possibilities of alternative sources of energy
  - green belt
  - organic farming.

2 Research

- The children should use libraries for research (for instance, to find out about the origin and administrative aspects of conservation areas) in addition to practical observation. Examples of the latter might be conducting a litter survey, or looking at the local environment to find buildings that are worth conserving.

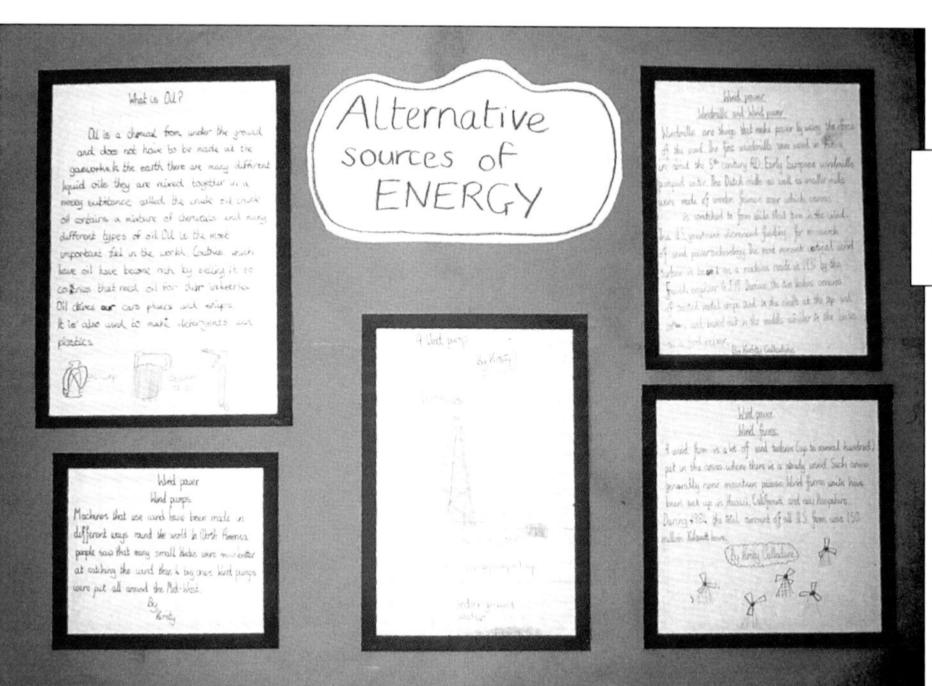

Kirsty researched alternative energy sources.

3 Writing to persuade

- The children should be encouraged to express their ideas about their chosen environmental issue in a variety of ways.

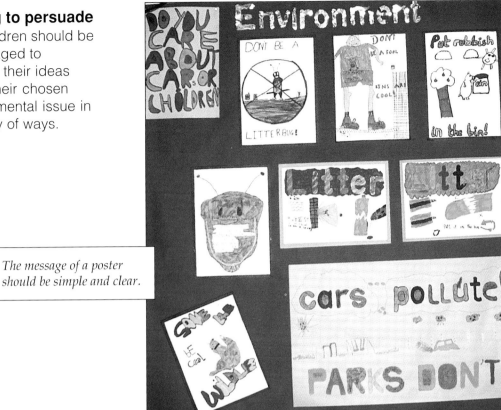

The message of a poster should be simple and clear.

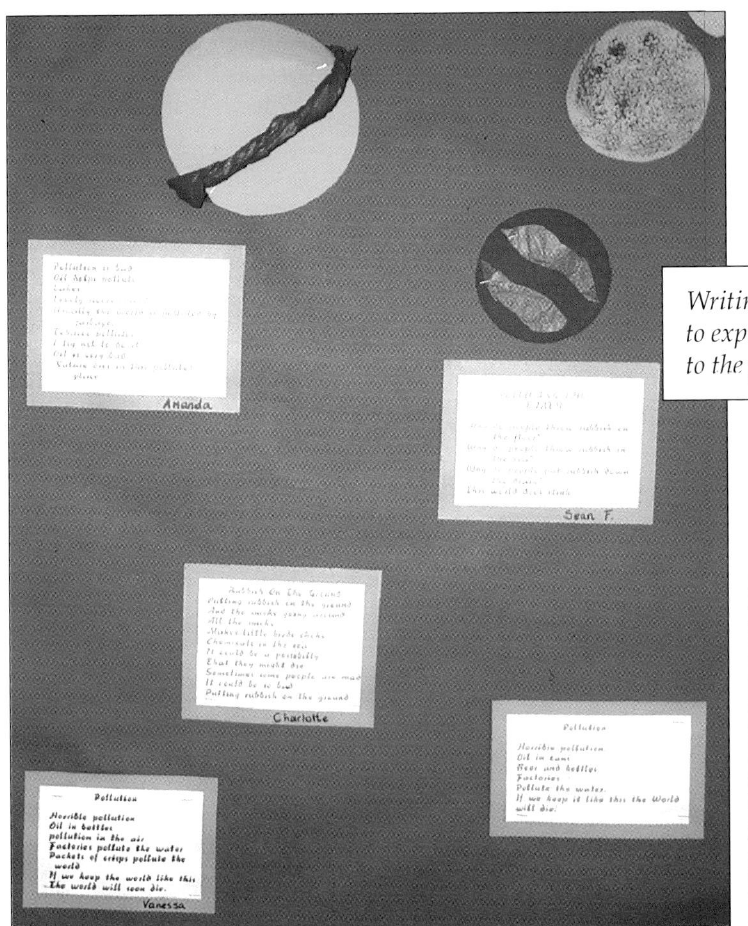

Writing poems allows the children to express their personal responses to the problem of pollution.

Extension activity

- Discuss the differences between an essay and a newspaper article. Both aim to persuade, but do so in different ways. Try to look at some newspaper articles on environmental issues.

Books

Organise a book week

Putting on a book week is one of the most effective ways of giving books and their authors a high profile and of raising interest and achievement in reading and writing. A well-organised book week can be an event that the children and their parents will remember for a long time.

Aims

- To give books a high profile.
- To encourage enjoyment in reading.
- To encourage the children to be book owners.
- To enable the children to see themselves as authors.

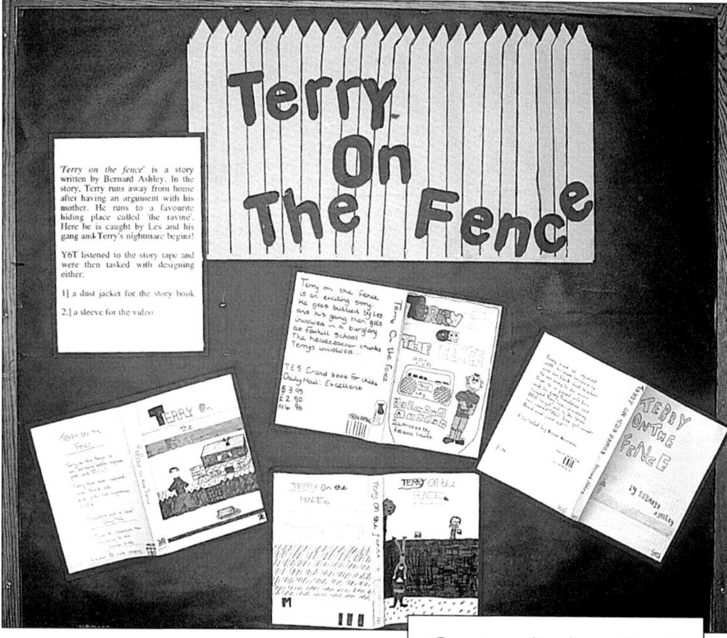

Create a display of book-related children's work.

1 Preparation

- To get the best out of a book week, make it a large-scale event:
  - Suspend the normal timetable and replace it entirely with book-related activities.
  - Involve all the staff and parents as readers, story-tellers, listeners and general helpers.
  - Flood the school with books. This will need to be budgeted for well in advance, but several publishers and booksellers operate a sale-or-return scheme.
  - Fill the school with posters and book-related displays.

2 What you need

- A budget. Hold fundraising activities, such as a sponsored read.
- Visitors. Try to have a published author. Alternatively, a local amateur could talk about the writing process.
- A range of writing and book-making materials.

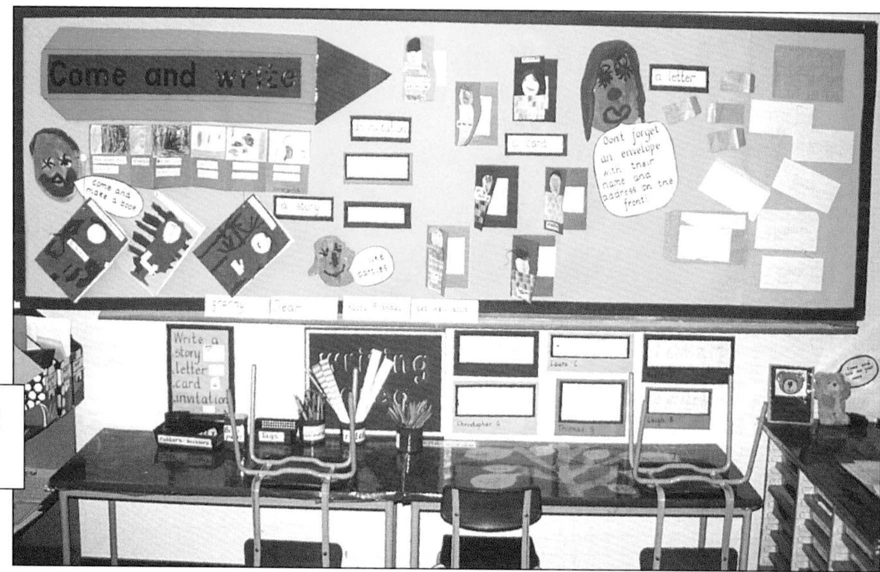

Set up a well-equipped writing area.

3 A school bookshop or club

- If you don't already have one of these, book week is a good time to start one.
- Stock pens, pencils, bookmarks and related novelty items. They make a good profit and act as a magnet to entice the children to the shop or club.

4 Preparations for an author visit

- There is nothing like the excitement of a visit from a 'real' writer to make a book week a memorable event. Regional arts associations should be able to help with contacts and possibly subsidies.
- Prepare by stocking up on the author's books and encouraging the children to read and respond to them in various ways. One way is to hold a competition about the author.
- Let the children prepare questions to ask the author during his or her visit.

During book week, hold a competition about a chosen author.

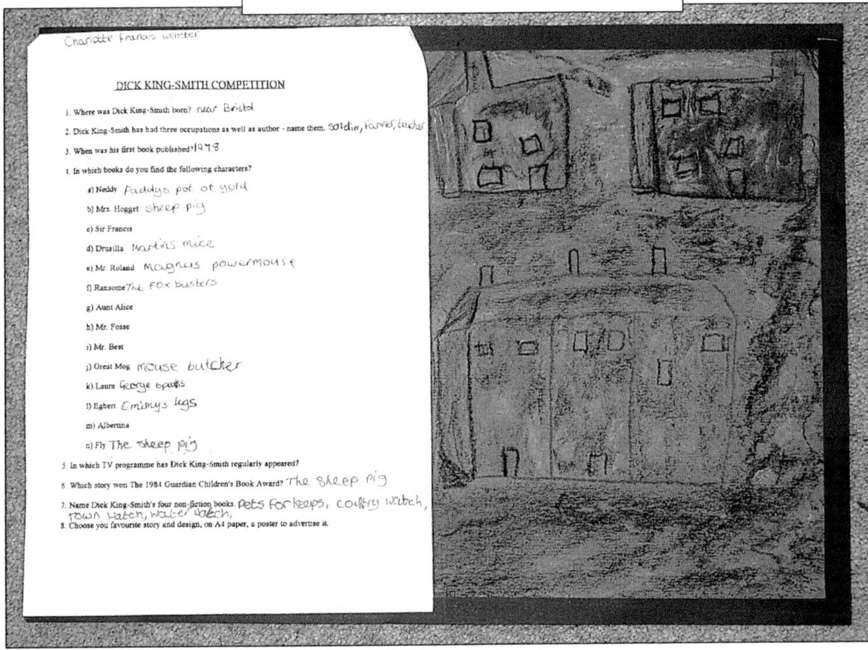

Charlotte Frances Webster

DICK KING-SMITH COMPETITION

1. Where was Dick King-Smith born? near Bristol
2. Dick King-Smith has had three occupations as well as author - name them. soldier, farmer, teacher
3. When was his first book published? 1978
4. In which books do you find the following characters?
   a) Neddy Paddys pot of gold
   b) Mrs. Hogget sheep pig
   c) Sir Francis
   d) Drusilla Martins mice
   e) Mr. Roland Magnus powermouse
   f) Ransome The Fox busters
   g) Aunt Alice
   h) Mr. Fosse
   i) Mr. Best
   j) Great Mog mouse butcher
   k) Laura George speaks
   l) Egbert Emilys legs
   m) Albertina
   n) Fly The sheep pig
5. In which TV programme has Dick King-Smith regularly appeared?
6. Which story won The 1984 Guardian Children's Book Award? The Sheep pig
7. Name Dick King-Smith's four non-fiction books. Pets for keeps, country watch, town watch, water watch,
8. Choose you favourite story and design, on A4 paper, a poster to advertise it.

5 Information technology

- Begin a library or class book area database. For example, a database on 'favourite books and where to find them' would be fun to set up and extremely useful for the future.

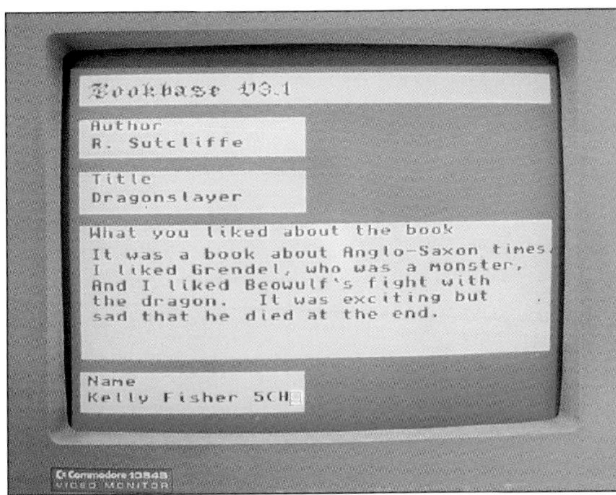

Children can input information under simple headings.

Extension activities

- Write letters of thanks to all involved.
- Continue the bookshop or book club and any other new activities, such as book databases.

Books

Book week activities

All the activities in which the children are involved throughout the week should be book-related. Ways of responding to books can range from making bookmarks to writing appreciations. Here are some suggestions. The emphasis should be on a fun approach.

Aims
- To encourage the children to read and respond creatively to books.
- To develop budding skills of literary appreciation, in a variety of enjoyable ways.

1 Book covers

- Before starting to make book covers, the children should study some real examples.
- They should make their covers as realistic as possible, featuring an illustration, the book title and the name of the author.
- On the back of the cover, they should include the 'blurb' – a brief synopsis of the book, information about the author and the price.
- They could make book covers to brighten up some of the older books in the school library.

Discuss what information appears on the front, back and spine of real covers and then let the children make their own.

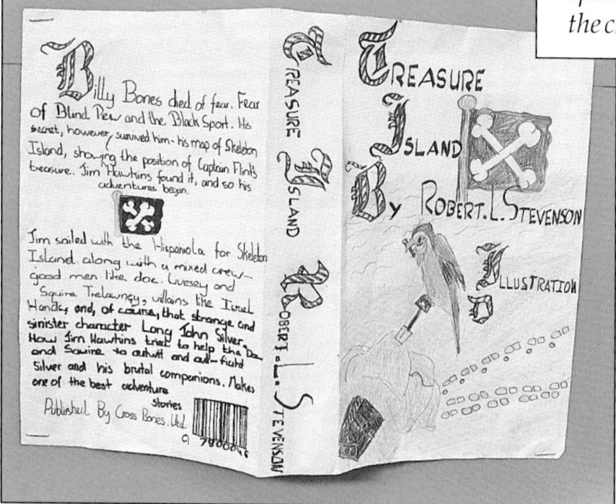

2 Posters

- The children could choose a book they have enjoyed and design a poster that will encourage others to read it.

3 Storyboards

- Working in pairs, the children could plan how to turn a favourite book into a sequence of scenes for a film.

The children could draw scenes like frames of a film.

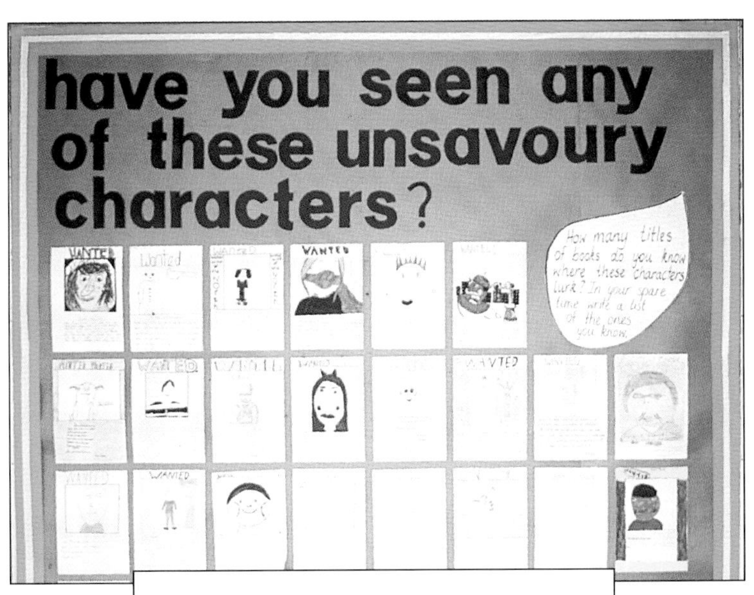

Make a display of unsavoury characters and invite other children to identify them.

4 Character studies

- The children could create a picture of their favourite character from a book.
- They could write a short character study to go with it.
- You could make a class display of a certain character type.

5 Information technology

- The children could turn a favourite book, for example *The Snow Queen,* into a computer adventure game. A number of paragraphs could simply be typed into a word processor. Each paragraph should be on a new page. The game could begin with a paragraph such as the following:
  'Start – Kay has been taken from Grandma's house by the Snow Queen and you have to try to find him. There are two roads leading from Grandma's house, one going east, the other going west; which direction will you choose?'
  Two paragraphs will then follow this – one headed 'east' and the other 'west'.

Turn a book into a computer adventure game.

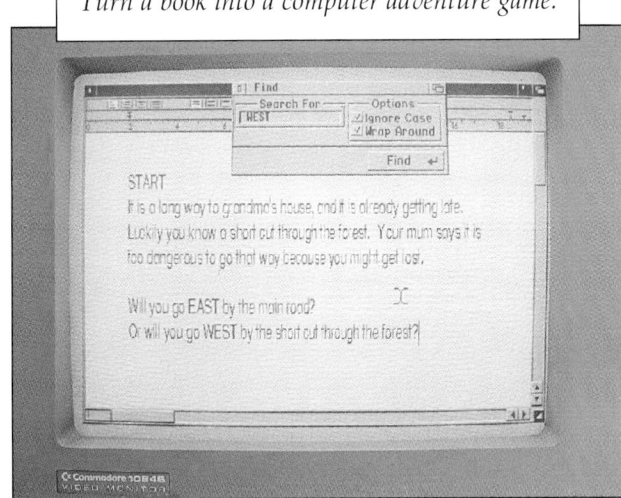

- Experiment with the pages that you have written. Display the first page, and make a choice. Use the 'search' or 'find' facility on your word processor and type in the keyword 'east' or 'west'. This will take you to the appropriate page. Note that all the keywords must be different.

Extension activities

- Make a time line for a book.
- Design a board game based on the plot of a book.
- Write a travel brochure about the setting of a book.
- Write a diary which a character in a book might have kept.
- 'Hot-seat' a character from a book.
- Turn a scene from a book into a play and act it out.
- Write a front-page article for a newspaper about something that happens in a book.
- Write a sequel to a book.

Making books

Like real authors, children derive tremendous satisfaction from seeing their writing presented in actual book form. Making books involves them not only in writing but also in practising art, craft and technology skills. Finished books can be displayed in the school or classroom library.

Aims

- To develop awareness of audience and purpose.
- To encourage neatness and accuracy.
- To encourage the children to see themselves as 'real' writers.

1 Preparation

- Find and display examples of different book formats, such as tall, wide, square, concertina and pop-up books. This will help the children to decide on a format for their own books.
- Look at the ways in which illustrations are presented on a page and at different types of illustration, such as photographs, drawings and diagrams.

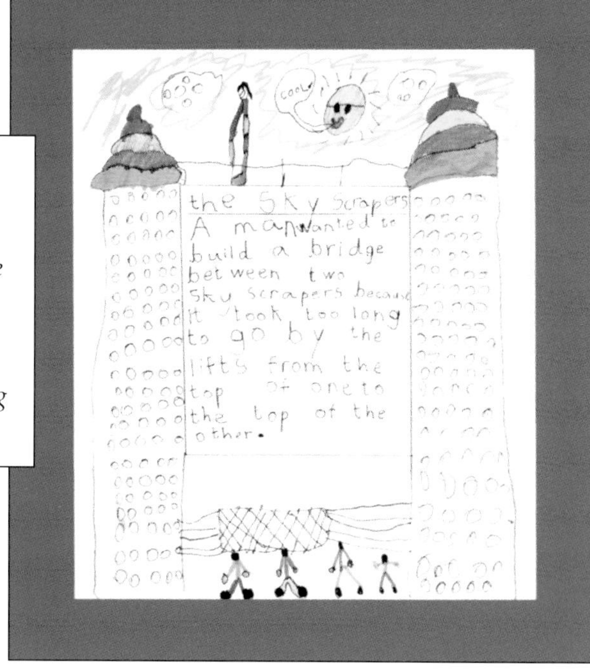

The children should write their story and redraft it before finally writing it out in their best writing and illustrating it.

2 Drafts

- The children's writing needs to be redrafted and proofread. They can then prepare the final copy, making it suitable in style and size for their chosen book format.

3 Creative ideas

- A simple and effective way to make a book without binding is to make it in a concertina form.
- A story could be presented on a scroll, turned by rollers inside a TV-shaped box.
- Collage covers for the books could be made. These are unusual and rewarding to make.

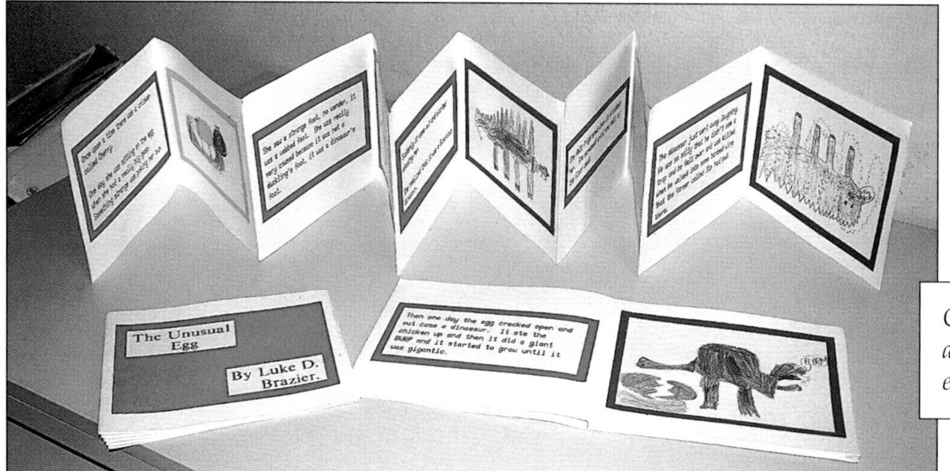

Concertina books are fun to make and easy to display.

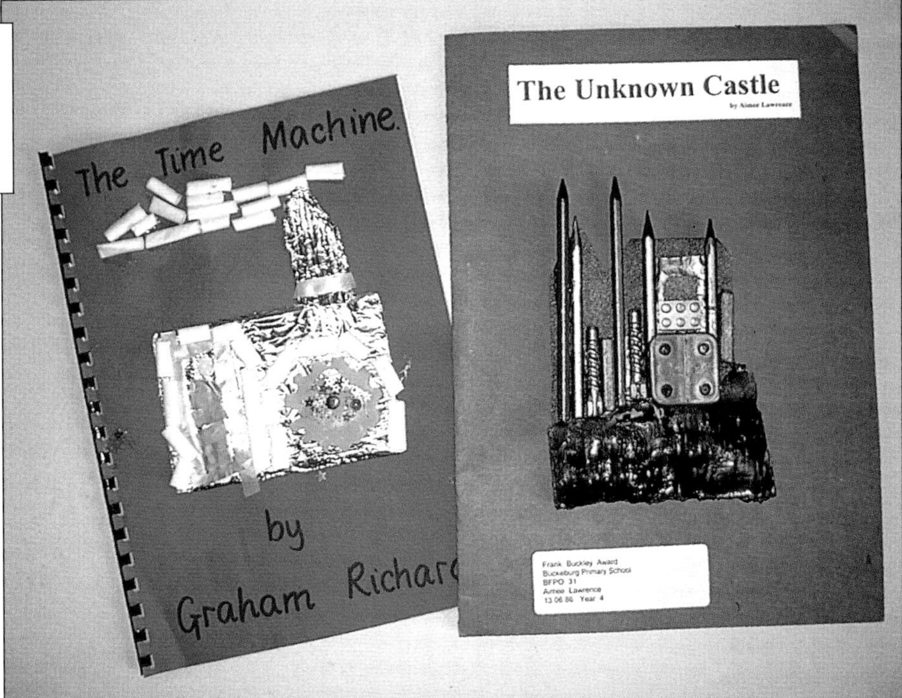

Collage covers are unusual and give books an added attraction.

The books can be bound using glue, staples or stitching. Other ideas include plastic binding strips or adapted ring-binders.

4 Information technology

- Word processors and desktop publishing programs enable the children to produce books that look as good as the real thing.

Extension activity

- Make a 'story box' – a decorated box that contains a range of stories and poems on a specific theme, such as 'giants'.

Researching newspapers

Children can learn a great deal from modelling the processes used in the production of newspapers and magazines. First they need to investigate what a newspaper contains and how it is presented.

Aims

To develop skills in:

- market research
- identifying and analysing different types of writing
- extending personal vocabulary.

Newspapers

1 Market research

- Ask the children to research which papers their families and other adults read and why they choose to read these particular ones. They might find that some people only buy one paper each week while others have one each day and two on Sundays. They should go on to draw some conclusions. Which was the most popular newspaper and why?

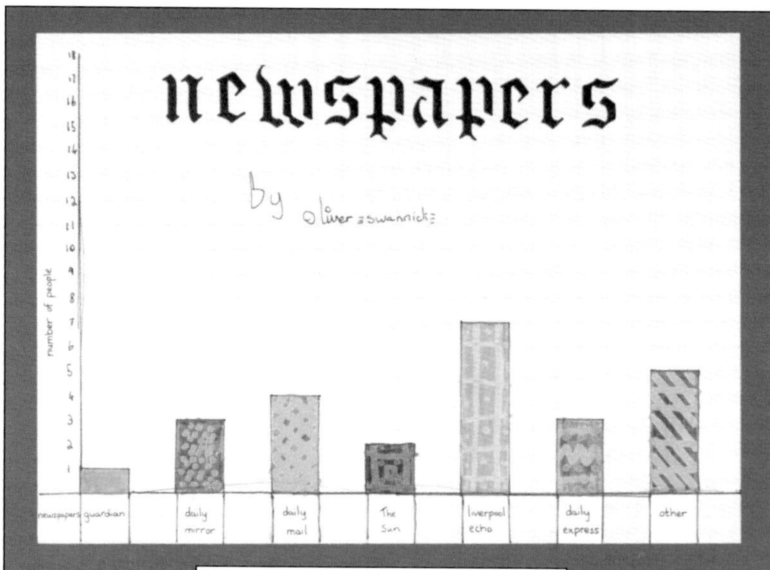

The children researched and recorded newspaper preference.

2 A detailed study

- Let the children study examples of newspapers and magazines. To help focus this investigation, ask them to:
  - look at the chosen newspaper and make a list of its contents
  - choose one page and sketch the page layout (draw the columns and boxes and note what is inside each)
  - study the different typefaces used and research the meanings of the terms 'serif', 'sans serif', 'bold' and 'italic'.

Types of articles in a newspaper

Sports
Jobs
Houses for sale
T.V Programmes for cable and sk
Stories
Puzzles and Competitions
Items for sale
Scratch and game cards
Horoscopes
Cartoon stories
Movie rentals
Help lines
Advetisements
Obituaries
Weather Forecastes
Annoucements – births – birthdays and marriages

By L Hendy

The children selected a newspaper and listed the different types of articles, pictures and other features that it contained.

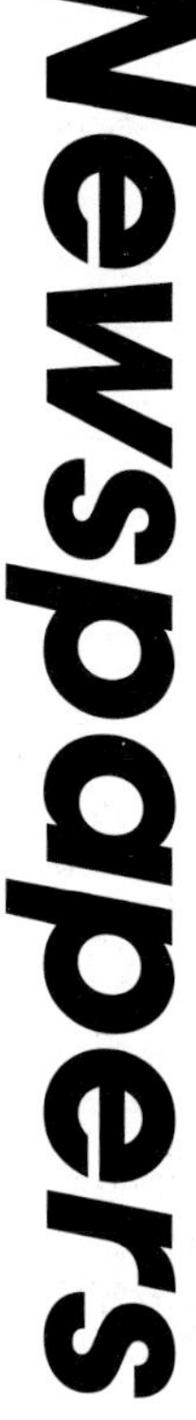

3 The language of newspapers

- Introduce some basic technical terms that the production team uses:
  - **body text** – the bulk of the writing
  - **caption** – explanatory words under a picture
  - **headline** – the main heading for a page or an article
  - **sub-headings** – smaller headings for each section
  - **intro** – the introductory paragraph after the headline that introduces the article
  - **typeface** – the name of the type used to print an article, for example 'Times'.

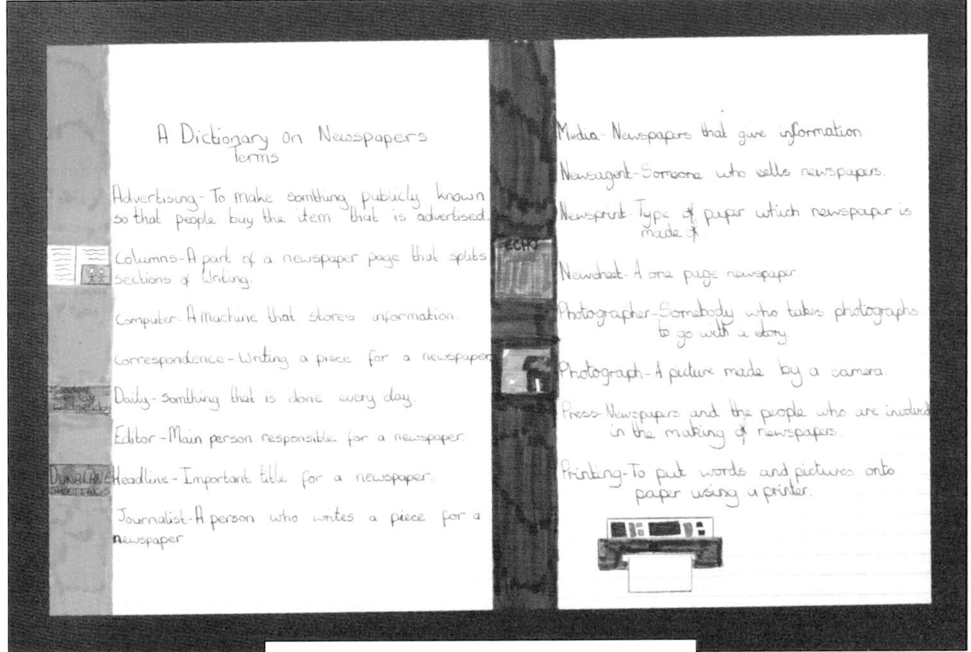

A Dictionary on Newspapers terms

Advertising- To make somthing publicly known so that people buy the item that is advertised.

Columns- A part of a newspaper page that splits sections of Writing.

Computer- A machine that stores information.

Correspondence- Writing a piece for a newspaper

Daily- somthing that is done every day.

Editor- Main person responsible for a newspaper.

Headline- Important title for a newspaper.

Journalist- A person who writes a piece for a newspaper

Media- Newspapers that give information.

Newsagent- Someone who sells newspapers.

Newsprint- Type of paper which newspaper is made of

Newsheet- A one page newspaper

Photographer- Somebody who takes photographs to go with a story

Photograph- A picture made by a camera.

Press- Newspapers and the people who are involved in the making of newspapers.

Printing- To put words and pictures onto paper using a printer.

The children created a dictionary of publishing terms for easy reference.

4 Journalists' jargon

- To make news reports sound dramatic, journalists use buzz words. The children could investigate which of these appear in their selected newspaper and make a display of them.

Word or phrase	Example
Drama	Head in closing school drama
Shock	Extra homework shock!
Horror	Playground litter horror!
Horror shock	Bones in basement horror shock!
Trauma	New pupil in bullying trauma
Saga	Extra homework saga continues
Nightmare	Detention nightmare
Bombshell	School rules bombshell!

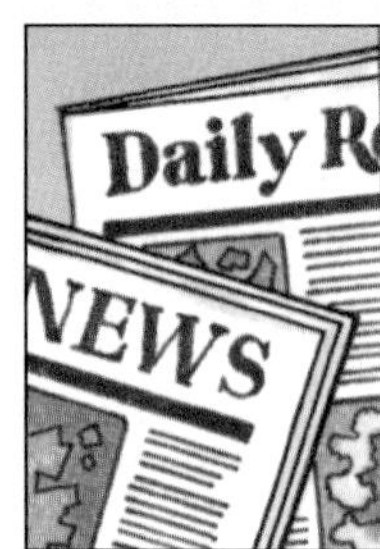

Newspapers

Editorial

The editorial processes require a considerable amount of writing. News writing must be accurate and up-to-date. This means that reporters and feature writers have to get out and about and make use of interviewing and note-taking skills. Later, they will have to rework their notes into readable news items. This is an ideal exercise for developing writing skills at an early age. The children should work in teams and take on the roles of those within a newspaper editorial office and produce their own newspaper.

Aims

To develop skills in:

- interviewing
- note-taking
- transcribing notes
- writing in journalistic style
- redrafting
- writing for an audience.

Interview with Mr. C. Hust about Election

How did you feel about Michael loosing the election?
I felt dissapointed but pleased for Neil.
Was it hard work convincing voters and advertising?
Yes because it had to be perfect. The speach didn't go to well.
Did you enjoy it?
Yes I learnt alot about group work, which is important.
Would you like to do it again?
Yes because I like group work.
Did you think publicity was important?
Yes because without publicity the voters would not get to know about the canditates.

Have you ever done this type of thing before
No
Mr Roderich came to talk to us did you learn alot
Yes, I learnt alot abot canvasing and advertising

By Kate Knight

One of the teachers had worked for a candidate in a local election, so Kate interviewed him about it.

1 Preparation

- Explain to the children the various roles in a newspaper editorial office of the:
  - editor
  - news reporters
  - feature writers
  - researchers.

2 The various roles

- The **news reporters** should report on the latest news. The **researchers** can help them with this. The team should discuss the news items it wishes to report on. These might include:
  - a forthcoming school event
  - new staff or staff who are leaving
  - school sports news
  - news of pupil achievements.
- The **editor** should then give each reporter a clear brief. They should all know what they are going to write about and who they are going to interview.

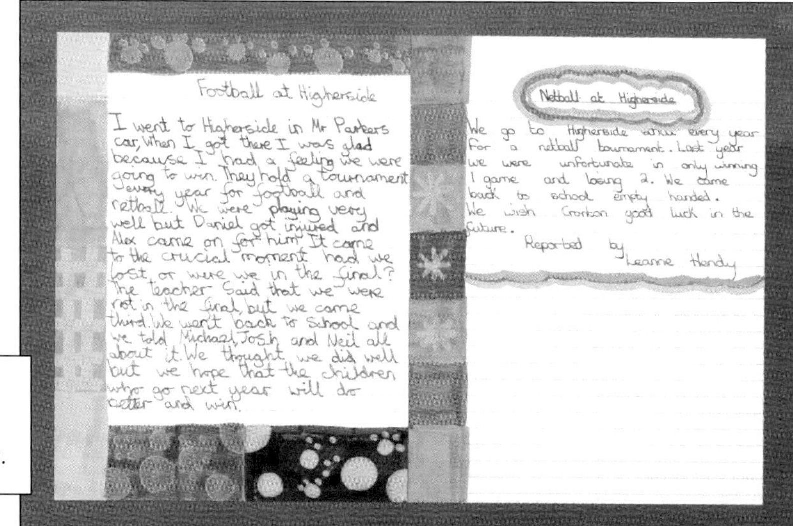
Football at Higherside

I went to Higherside in Mr Parkers car, When I got there I was glad because I had a feeling we were going to win. They hold a tournament every year for football and netball. We were playing very well but Daniel got injured and Alex came on for him. It came to the crucial moment had we lost or were we in the final? The teacher Said that we were not in the final, but we came third. We went back to School and we told Michael, Josh and Neil all about it. We thought we did well but we hope that the children who go next year will do better and win.

Netball at Higherside

We go to Higherside [illegible] every year for a netball tournament. Last year we were unfortunate in only winning 1 game and losing 2. We came back to school empty handed. We wish Cronton good luck in the future.

Reported by Leanne Hendy

The children were allocated different stories to investigate.

3 Interviewing

- Before interviewing someone, the children should jot down three or four key questions to ask. These will guide the interview but need not be stuck to rigidly. Advise the children to make notes during the interview, but not to let the writing interfere with the conversation. Help them to practise interviewing and note-taking. They could take it in turns to interview each other and make notes. Many reporters use shorthand. They could experiment with ways of shortening words, such as:
  - using consonants only
  - abbreviating
  - symbols.

4 Interview writing

- As soon as possible after the interview, the children should write a first draft, bearing their audience in mind. If they need help, they should consult the editor. They should then present their final version to the **production team** (see pages 28 and 29).

The feature writers provided some excellent articles and 'filler' items.

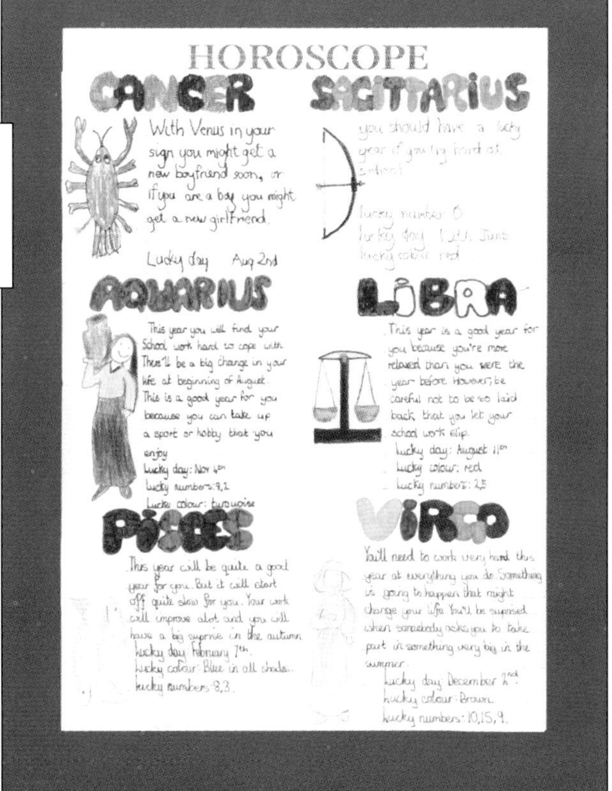

HOROSCOPE

CANCER

With Venus in your sign you might get a new boyfriend soon, or if you are a boy you might get a new girlfriend.

Lucky day Aug 2nd

SAGITTARIUS

AQUARIUS

This year you will find your School work hard to cope with. There'll be a big change in your life at beginning of August. This is a good year for you because you can take up a sport or hobby that you enjoy

Lucky day: Nov 4th
Lucky numbers: 9,2
Lucky colour: turquoise

LIBRA

This year is a good year for you because you're more relaxed than you were the year before. However, be careful not to be so laid back that you let your school work slip.

lucky day: August 11th
Lucky colour: red
Lucky numbers: 2,5

PISCES

This year will be quite a good year for you. But it will start off quite slow for you. Your work will improve alot and you will have a big surprise in the autumn.

lucky day February 7th.
lucky colour Blue in all shades.
lucky numbers 8,3.

VIRGO

You'll need to work very hard this year at everything you do. Something is going to happen that might change your life. You'll be suprised when somebody asks you to take part in something very big in the summer.

lucky day December 2nd.
lucky colour: Brown.
lucky numbers: 10,15,9.

5 Feature writing

- The feature writers should provide a range of articles on different subjects, as well as 'fillers' such as quizzes, crosswords and horoscopes.

Extension activities

- Everyone should contribute something. Some extra ideas are:
  - a joke page
  - letters to the editor
  - problems for the problem page
  - advertisements.

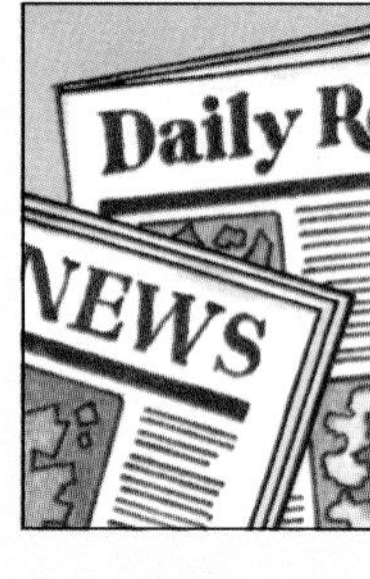

Production processes

The way in which newspapers and magazines are produced in the classroom depends very much on the resources that are available, but the main principle should not be sacrificed – the classroom newspaper should be modelled as closely as possible on its real counterpart.

Aims

To develop skills in:

- making a final product
- working as a team
- effective use of information technology and art materials
- using appropriate technical terms.

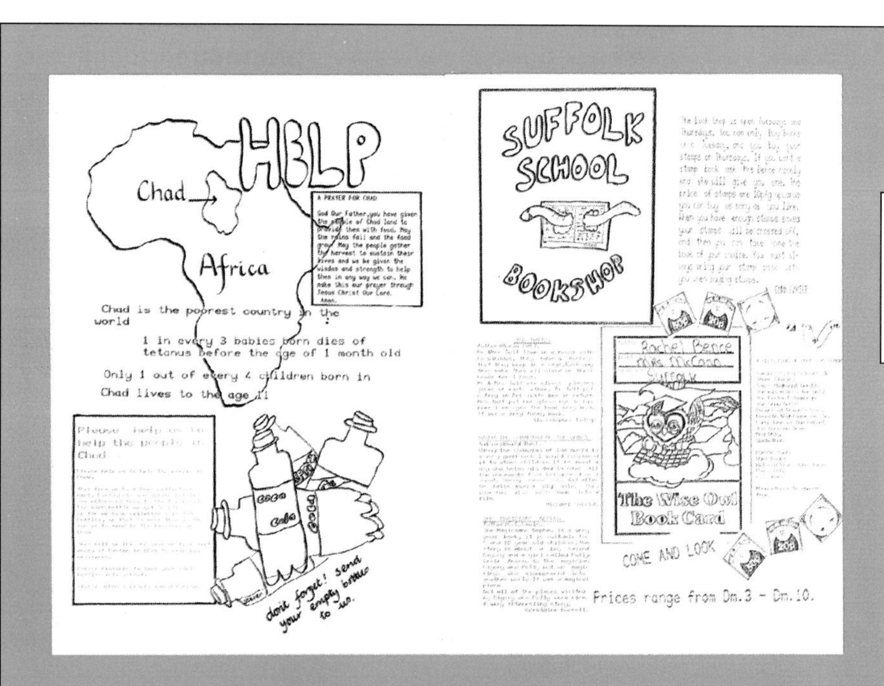

The final product – a class newspaper that was put together by the various teams.

1 Team briefing

- Explain to the children how the work of producing newspapers is organised. The **production team** comprises three groups:
  - **proofreaders**, who check grammar, spelling and factual accuracy
  - **illustrators/ photographers**, who draw pictures, make photocopies or take photographs
  - **layout artists**, who design the page layout and assemble the various pieces to make up the final pages.

2 Allocating the jobs

- Organise the children into groups, if possible giving jobs in areas where the children have talents. For example, those children who enjoy reading can be the **proofreaders** and those who enjoy drawing can be the **illustrators**.

3 Information technology

- The children could create headlines and sub-headings using a computer. They could also word-process some or all of the articles.
- Some desktop publishing programs have been designed for use by children and can replace manual cut-and-paste.
- The children could use a camera (a Polaroid is ideal because of its instant results) so that the pictures in the newspaper are actual photographs of the people and places in the articles.

4 Putting the newspaper together

- The **news team** and **features team** should submit their copy either word-processed or written as neatly as possible in columns. More able children should be able to write in 9cm columns (three columns per A3 sheet). Younger children may be happier with wider columns of 13cm (two per A3 sheet).
- The articles are then checked by the **proofreaders**, and corrections are made if necessary.
- The **illustrators** and **photographers** provide pictures to go with some of the articles. (The **editor** has the final decision on which articles are to be illustrated.)
- The articles are cut up into sections to be pieced together with pictures, headings and so on, by the **layout artists**. Headlines can be written with a thick felt-tipped pen.

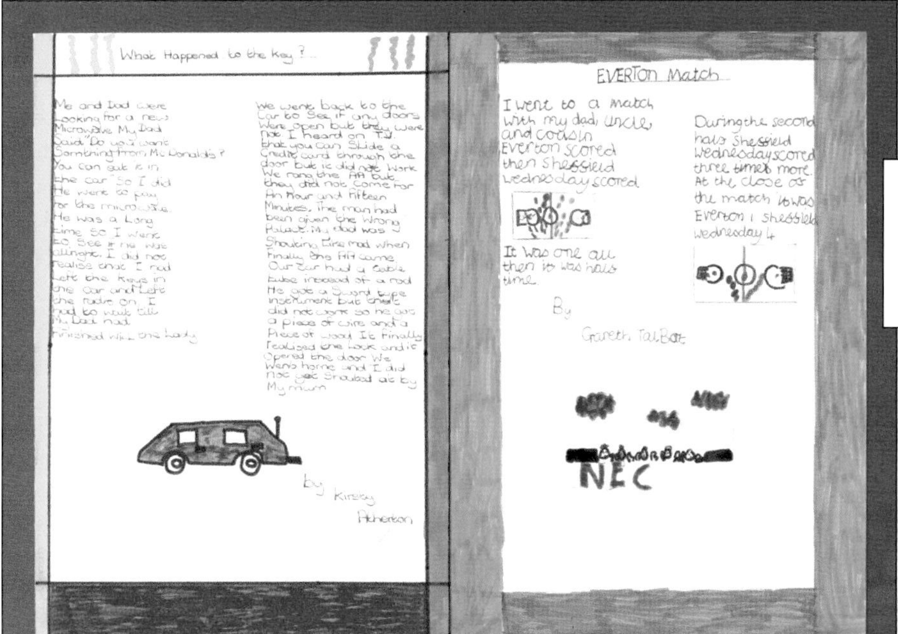

What Happened to the Key ?...

Me and Dad were Looking for a new Microwave. My Dad Said "Do you want Somthing from McDonalds? You can eat it in the car" So I did. He went to pay for the microwave. He was a Long time so I went to See if he was allright. I did not realise that I had Left the keys in the car and Left the radio on. I had to wait till My Dad had finished with the Lady

We went back to the Car to See if any doors were open but they were not. I heard on T.V. that you can Slide a Credit card through the door but it did not work. We rang the AA but they did not Come for An Hour and fifteen Minutes. The man had been given the Wrong Palace. My dad was Shouting the mad when finally the AA came. Our Car had a Cable tube instead of a rod. He got a Sword type instrument but that did not work so he got a piece of wire and a Piece of wood. It finally realised the Lock and it opened the door. We went home and I did not get Shouted at by My mum

by Kirsty Atherton

EVERTON Match

I went to a match with my dad, uncle, and cousin. Everton scored then Sheffield Wednesday scored.

It was one all then it was half time.

During the second half Sheffield Wednesday scored three times more. At the close of the match it was Everton 1 Sheffield Wednesday 4

By Gareth Talbot

NEC

The writers produced their stories in their best writing, formatted into columns.

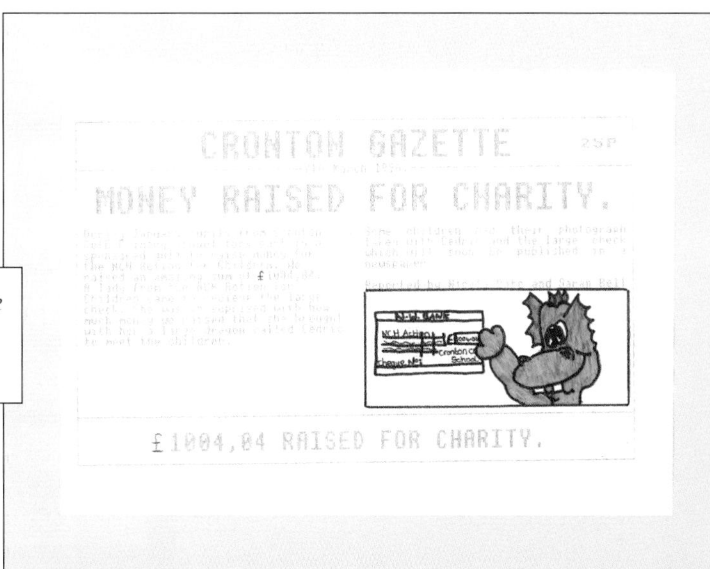

CRONTON GAZETTE 25P

MONEY RAISED FOR CHARITY.

Reported by Nicola [illegible] and Sarah Bell

£1004,04 RAISED FOR CHARITY.

The layout artists put the writing and pictures together.

Investigating homes

A topic on homes could begin with an investigation of the different types of buildings that are used as homes, what they are made from and how many people live in them. While most children live in houses, many others live in other types of dwellings, such as caravans. You could go on to look at different types of homes around the world.

Aims
- To research information about houses and homes.
- To find methods of recording findings.

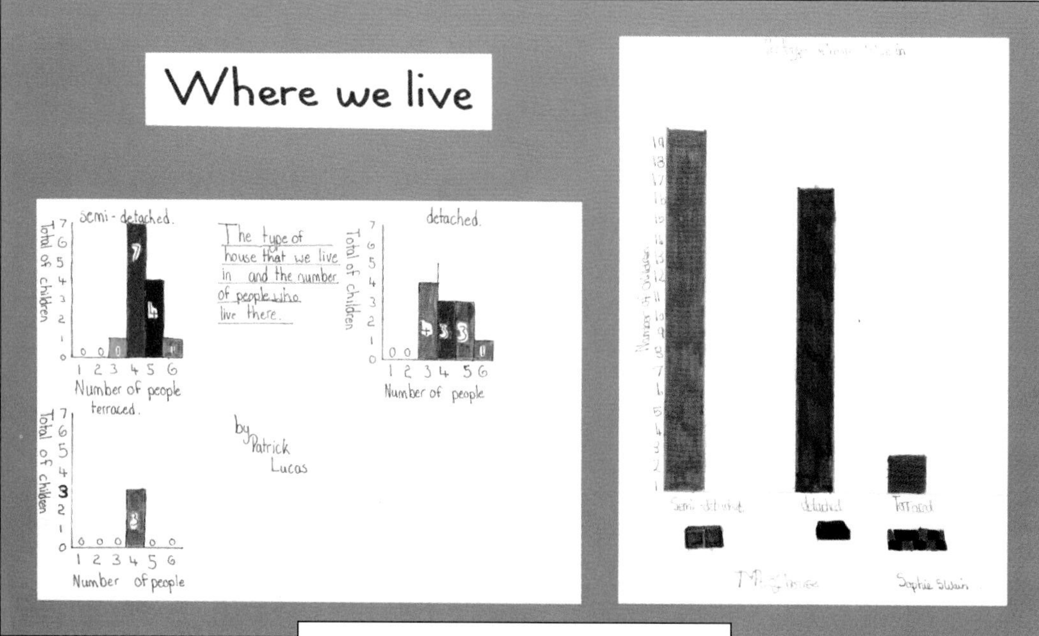

The children recorded their findings on the types of homes in their locality.

1 Preparation

- Ask the children to look at the different types of homes in their own locality. They should make notes on the following:
  - different types of homes, such as houses, flats, caravans and barges
  - the different types within one category, such as terraced, semi-detached or detached
  - the types of materials that were used in the construction of these houses
  - whether or not they have gardens.

2 Recording their findings

- The children could make graphs to show the different types of houses that they have noted.
- They could also survey the houses in their immediate area and find out the average number of people who live in them.

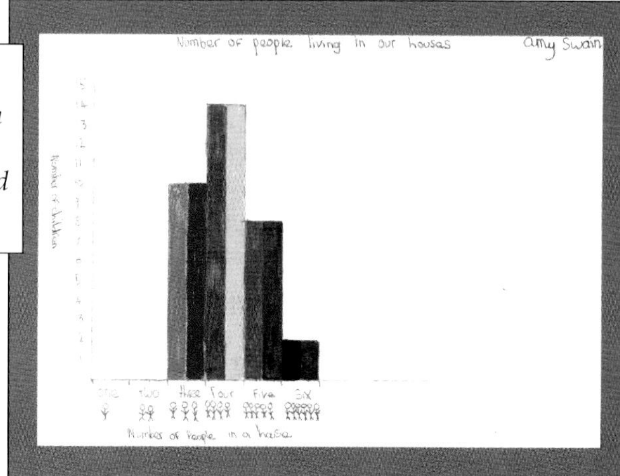

Some children concentrated on the number of people who lived in one house.

3 Materials used in houses

- The children could look at their own homes or those of other people and find out all the different materials that were used in their construction.
- They could compare this with other types of homes, such as caravans and flats.
- They could then look at materials used to build houses in other parts of the world.

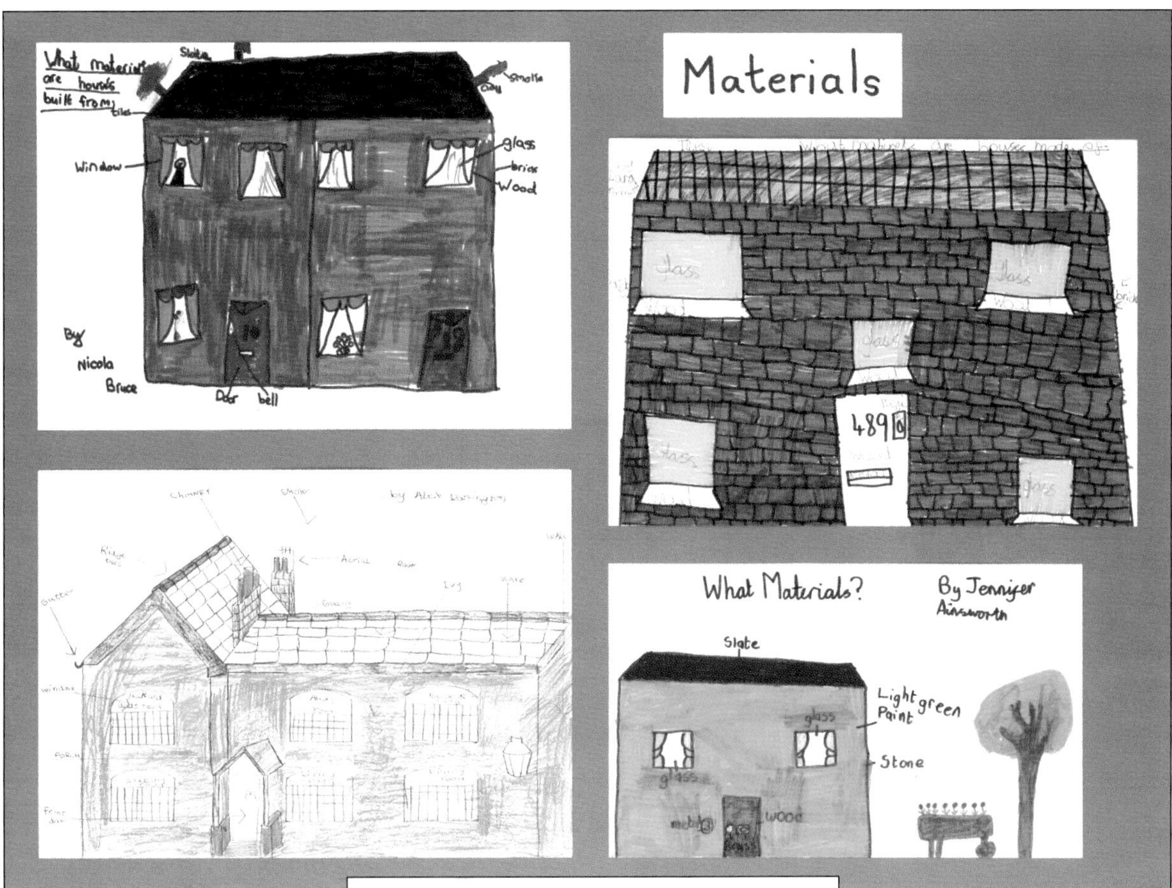

The children drew their houses and labelled the different materials that had been used in their construction.

Extension activities

- Design an ideal home. Begin by making a list of all the different rooms. Plan sensible positions for windows, doorways, lights and power points.
- Le Corbusier said 'a house is a machine for living in'. Design a house for the next century with lots of modern inventions to make life easier.
- Use a computer to design a house. This can be done in a simple way using a painting or drawing program, but specialist programs such as *My World 2 – Technology and Design Home* are also available (Semerc software).

Homes

Safety in the home

It is important for the children to think about safety, particularly in the home, since this is where most accidents happen. Clear and persuasive writing about this issue can help to save lives.

Aims
- To develop clear communication, using a combination of words and diagrams.
- To learn how to write persuasively.

1 Preparation

- Begin with a discussion on safety in the home. This is most effective if the children start to talk about the subject in groups and then report back to the whole class. Some particular topics for them to consider are:
  - gas and electrical equipment
  - first aid
  - fire precautions and fire fighting
  - small children
  - dangerous furniture, fittings and carpets.

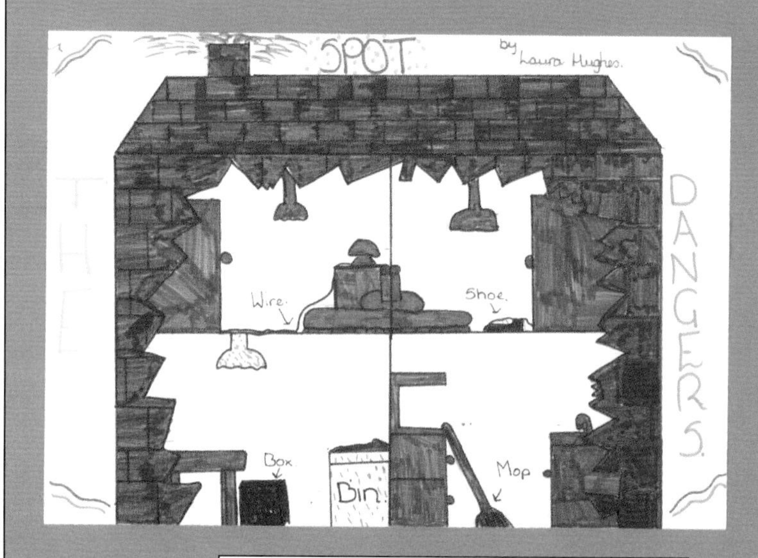

The children drew and labelled plans of their homes. They then marked the places that they felt could be danger spots.

DANGER

An Accident in the home.

One day my older Sister was chasing me around the house. So I ran into the living room. As I was running into the room I knocked the door out of the way and it hit the ironing board. The ironing board tillted and the iron fell off. Christine was on the chair but it missed her and it never made a mark on the chair. We were all in Shock. I did not get shouted at but it was very daft of me.

The children wrote about some of the accidents in the home that they had heard about.

2 Making plans

- Ask the children to draw a large plan of a house and garage and to label the danger points in each room. This could be done in groups, with each child in the group responsible for labelling a separate room.

3 Research

- The children could ask their parents about any accidents in the home that they can remember or have heard about. The children could then look around their own home to:
  - find examples of safety notices (on plugs, electrical equipment and gas boilers)
  - identify any danger points.

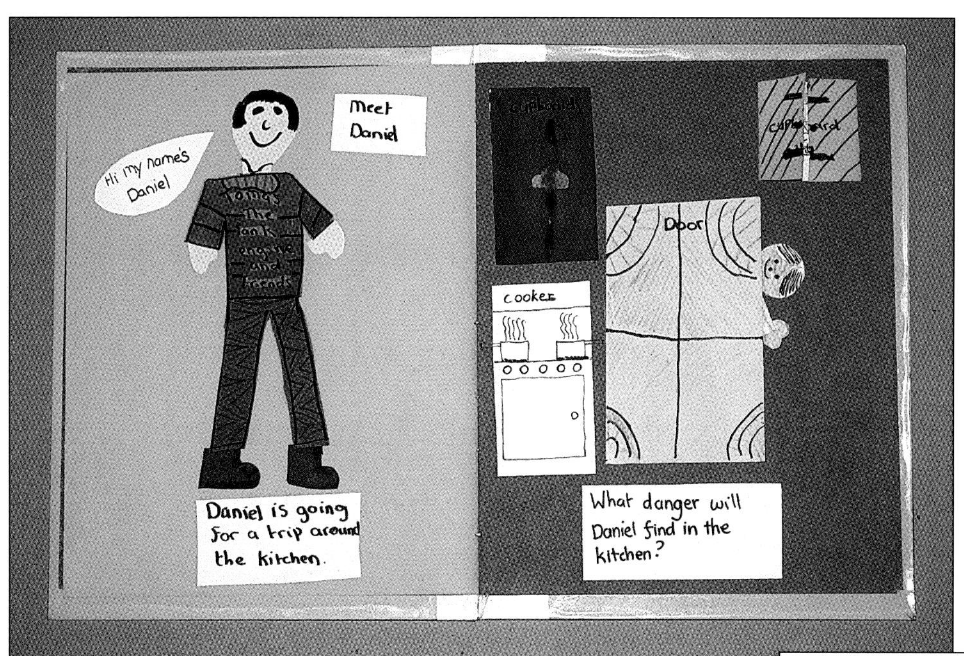

One child made a book with lifting flaps and other interactive features to show the dangers Daniel faces at home.

4 Safety campaign

- The children could devise a safety campaign, focusing on the home. They might include the following types of material:
  - posters and leaflets
  - slogans and logos
  - designs for a T-shirt or badge
  - lists
  - charts and diagrams.

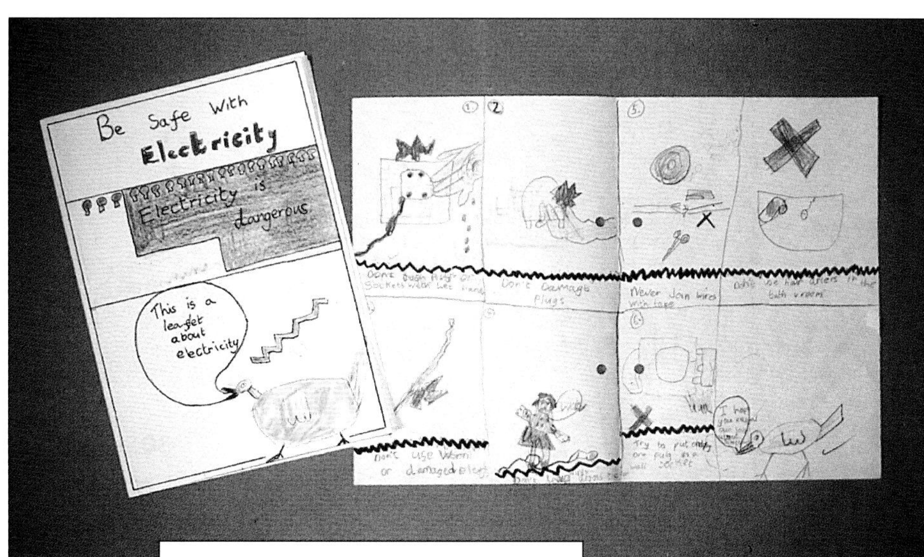

A leaflet with clear pictures can cover a range of safety issues in detail.

5 Information technology

- Most databases have a facility that enables data to be presented as a bar graph. Ask the children to do some research into different kinds of accidents in the home and display them as a graph. The graphs can be used in their posters and leaflets.

Extension activity

- Encourage the children to share their work with parents to try to improve some aspects of safety in their homes.

Selling a home

The children may have experienced selling a home or moving to a new home. An interesting activity is to describe a home first, from a personal point of view, as somewhere to live, and then as a property to sell.

Aim

- To write different kinds of description for different purposes and audiences.

The children made labelled drawings of their houses.

They also produced written descriptions of their homes.

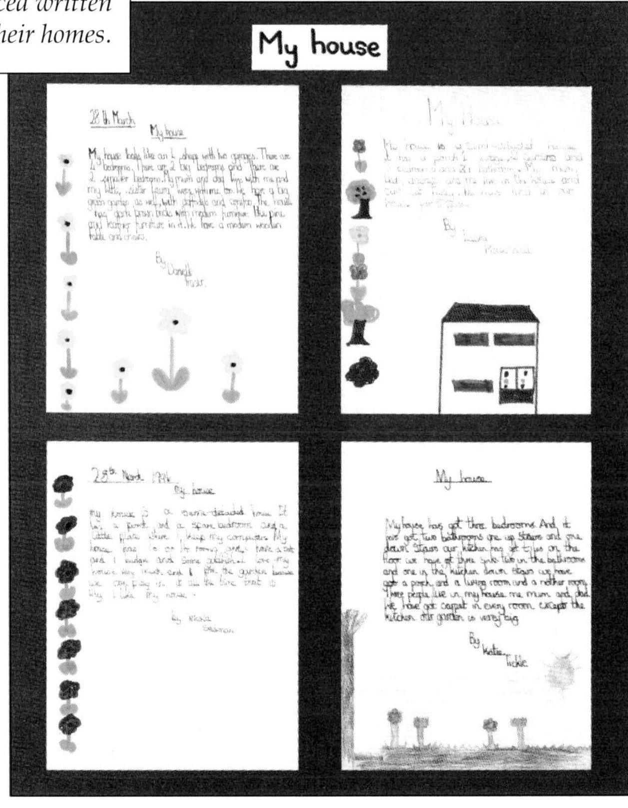

1 Preparation

- Ask the children to:
  - look at the property pages in the local newspaper
  - draw an annotated plan of their home (some children might feel more comfortable drawing the home of a relative or friend, a former home or an ideal home)
  - draw a plan of the garden, including any outbuildings, such as a shed or a garage
  - sketch the front view and the various rooms
  - write about their homes – what they like or hate about them.

Homes

2 Simulation

- Organise the children into small groups for an 'estate agent simulation'. Each group pretends that it is an estate agency. They pool all of their plans, sketches and descriptions done at the 'preparation' stage and start to set themselves up as an estate agency by doing the following:
  - deciding a price for each house
  - designing a leaflet to advertise each house
  - producing a leaflet giving brief details of all the houses.

3 Information technology

- Some children could enter the details of each house on to a database. They should be able to retrieve information about each house quickly, at the request of a client.
- Others could enter the information in the style of a typical estate agent's information sheet. These could be printed out and other information added to them, such as photographs or plans of the house.

Some children created a database on the computer. The information was then available upon request.

Some groups put the information on to computers and produced realistic information sheets.

MANOR SCHOOL
ESTATE AGENTS

FOR SALE: 112 CHURCH STREET

DESCRIPTION OF HOUSE

This house is a semi-detached house. There is an old tin garage at the side. The house could do with repainting but it has recently been double glazed. There are large gardens at the front and at the back. The back garden goes straight out onto woodland. 3 bedrooms.

PLAN OF GROUND FLOOR

dining room, lounge, kitchen, hall, WC

PLAN OF FIRST FLOOR

bedroom 1, bedroom 2, bedroom 3, bathroom, WC

PRICE: £55,000

If you would like to find out more about the house please come to Mrs Ford's classroom at 12.30.

MANOR SCHOOL
ESTATE AGENTS

DESCRIPTION OF THE HOUSE

This is a large detached house with a beastiful ivy-covered front. There is a garage for one car at the side of the house. At the other side is a garden shed. You can see from the picture that the house has been double glazed with white PVC. 4 bedrooms.

DESCRIPTION OF THE GARDEN

The front garden is open plan. The back garden is quiet big and there are some roses and shrubs. The garden is private. There are large trees at the back.

GROUND FLOOR PLAN

lounge, dining room, study, hall, wc, kitchen

UPSTAIRS PLAN

bedroom 1, bed room 4, bedroom 2, bath-room, landing, wc, bedroom 3

PRICE: £80.000

If you would like to look at the house, please come to Mrs Ford's classroom at 12.30.!

Recording the weather

The subject of the weather gives rise to a variety of writing. Weather observations need to be recorded accurately and precisely. The data is then analysed and useful conclusions drawn. Finally, these conclusions need to be presented in a way that people can understand, in a weather forecast (pages 38–39).

Aims

- To develop accurate observation and recording.
- To draw conclusions from data.

1 Preparation

- Let the children work in groups of about four or five. They should record the local weather over a period of a few days. The groups can compare the weather data they collect and present their findings to each other. It will be interesting to see whether they agree.

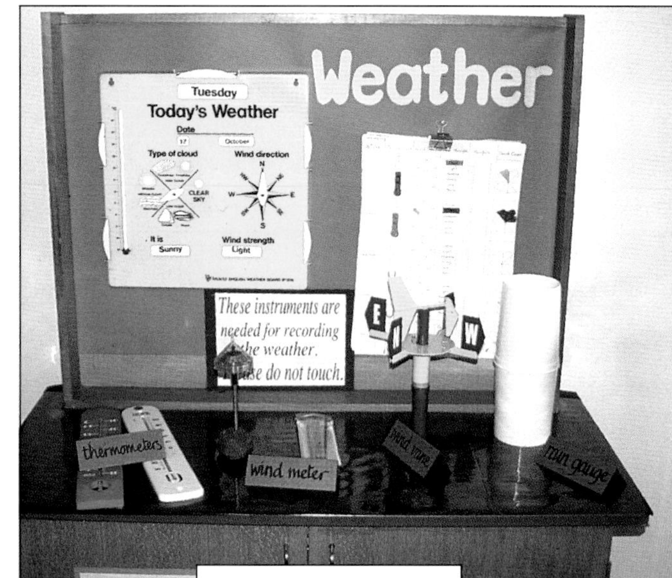

A display of weather recording equipment.

One group kept a detailed chart of the weather for a week.

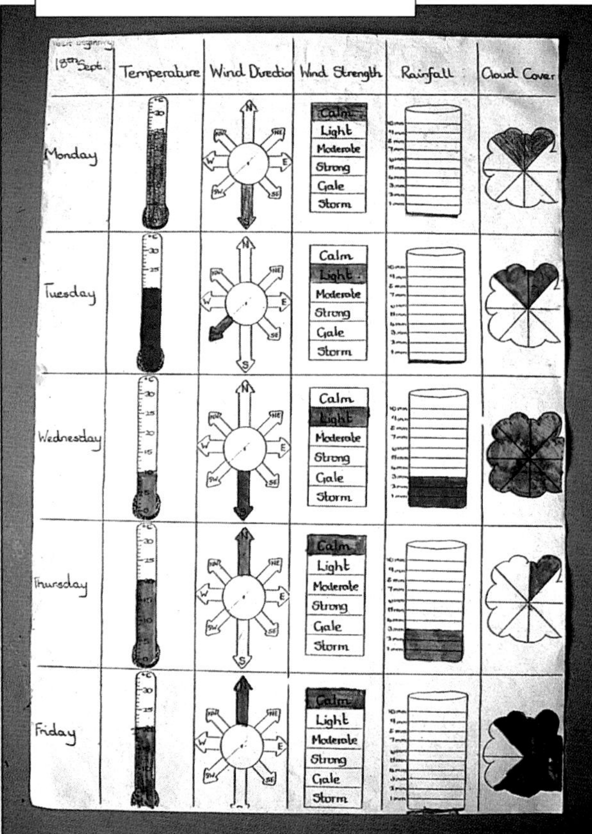

- One of the main sources of data will be a 'weather station'. Depending on the equipment available and the age range of the children, this might include:
  - a barometer
  - a thermometer
  - a wind vane
  - a rain gauge
  - an anemometer.

  The last three can be made from simple materials.
- The children should also study cloud formations and the effects of wind on the landscape (the latter possibly linked with work on the Beaufort scale).
- They could interview their parents and other adults about 'weather lore'.

2 Recording

- In addition to the charts and graphs that record statistics, the children could also record the weather in other ways:
  - They could keep weather diaries, recording detailed observations about relevant subjects, for instance the way animals or plants are behaving.
  - They could sketch clouds and the effect of the wind on smoke, litter, trees and so on.
  - They could research popular weather lore and find out how much truth there is in these sayings.

Weather diaries and sketches are useful for keeping a record of the weather.

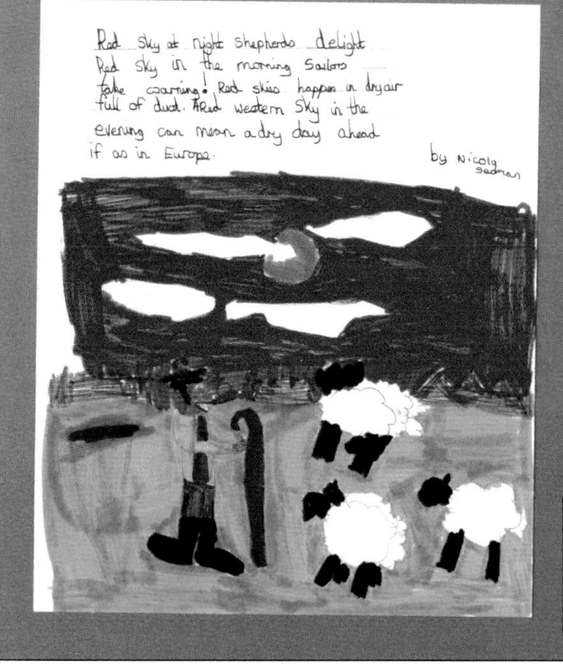

3 Analysing the data

- The groups could then meet to study the data they have collected. They should try to answer the question: 'What are the signs that show that it will be cold (or rainy, sunny and so on)?' They could compare their findings with some of the weather lore that they have researched and consider how accurate weather lore can be. They could use this information to make a forecast chart for easy reference.

The children used a variety of information to predict the weather.

Extension activity

The Meteorological Office was one of the first organisations to use computers to make sense of all the complicated data that weather stations collect. One group of children could enter their data into a database or a weather forecast program.

Weather forecasts

Aims

- To learn to communicate complex data clearly.
- To exploit the potential of different media.

Recording and analysing data are only a part of what meteorologists do. It is also their job to communicate their forecasts to the general public. Weather forecasts are presented in different ways in different media. Before the children start work, let them watch, read and listen to several weather forecasts and then discuss them.

1 Preparation

- Each group could be asked to choose one of the following ways in which to present a weather forecast:
  - as on television
  - as in a newspaper
  - as on radio.
- The groups should then work out the main points of their forecast and plan how to present it clearly to the intended audience.

One group collected weather reports from different newspapers and wrote what they thought of them.

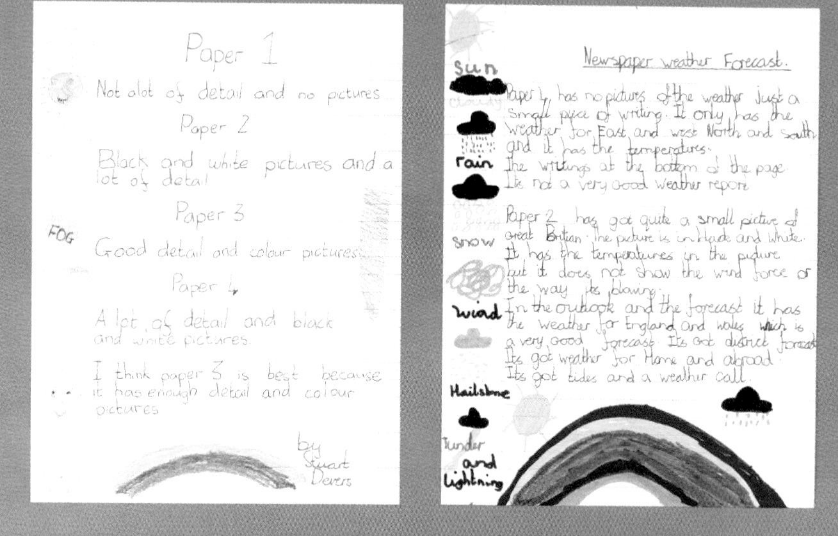

Paper 1
Not alot of detail and no pictures
Paper 2
Black and white pictures and a lot of detail
Paper 3
Good detail and colour pictures
Paper 4
A lot of detail and black and white pictures
I think paper 3 is best because it has enough detail and colour pictures
by Stuart Devers

Newspaper weather Forecast.
Paper 1 has no pictures of the weather just a small piece of writing. It only has the weather for East and west North and south and it has the temperatures. The writings at the bottom of the page Its not a very good weather report.
Paper 2 has got quite a small picture of Great Britian. The picture is in black and white. It has the temperatures in the picture but it does not show the wind force or the way its blowing. In the outlook and the forecast it has the weather for England and wales which is a very good forecast. Its got district forecast Its got weather for Home and abroad Its got tides and a weather call.

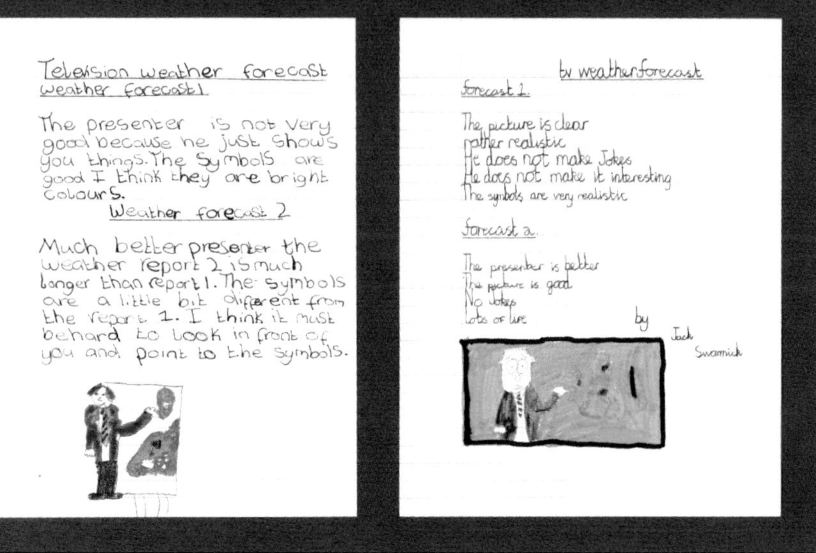

Television weather forecast
weather forecast 1
The presenter is not very good because he just shows you things. The symbols are good I think they are bright colours.
Weather forecast 2
Much better presenter the weather report 2 is much longer than report 1. The symbols are a little bit different from the report 1. I think it must be hard to look in front of you and point to the symbols.

tv weatherforecast
forecast 1.
The picture is clear
rather realistic
He does not make Jokes
He does not make it interesting
The symbols are very realistic
forecast 2.
The presenter is better
The picture is good
No Jokes
Lots of [illegible]
by Jack [illegible]

Another group watched the weather forecast on television and made notes on content, pictures and style of presentation, including any jokes the presenter made.

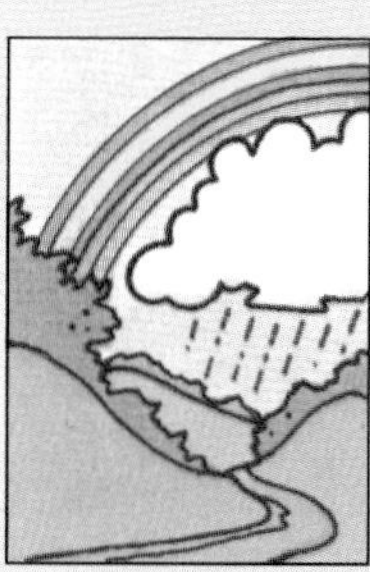

2 Presenting the weather

- Each group should present its weather forecast to the whole class.
- **A weather forecast for radio**
  While listening to weather reports on the radio, the children should make notes on how they are presented. They should then write the script for their own presentation, ending with a summary of the main points.
- **A television presentation**
  Use a large wall map or, if possible, an overhead projector. The main acetate sheet will show a map which the children have coloured and labelled. Smaller pieces of acetate with drawings of clouds and so on can be used to show weather conditions.
- **A newspaper item**
  Newspaper weather forecasts usually include a map. The children should draw a map and include simple symbols for types of weather. The report should also contain a brief report for each of the different geographical areas in the UK.

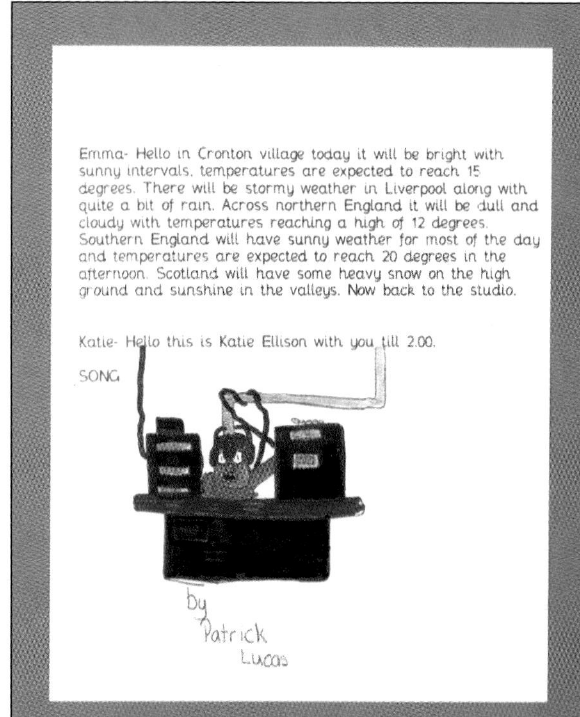

Emma- Hello in Cronton village today it will be bright with sunny intervals, temperatures are expected to reach 15 degrees. There will be stormy weather in Liverpool along with quite a bit of rain. Across northern England it will be dull and cloudy with temperatures reaching a high of 12 degrees. Southern England will have sunny weather for most of the day and temperatures are expected to reach 20 degrees in the afternoon. Scotland will have some heavy snow on the high ground and sunshine in the valleys. Now back to the studio.

Katie- Hello this is Katie Ellison with you till 2.00.

SONG

by Patrick Lucas

One group's script for a radio weather forecast.

Newspaper weather forecast.

Up in the scottish islands it will rain the temperatures will reach 5 degrees. AT the top of scotland it will snow temperatures will reach minus 4 degrees. In the Midlands it will rain temperatures will reach 3 degrees. In the East it will snow and temperatures will reach 0 degrees. Wales will have snow and will reach temperatures of -1. In the south of England there will be sunny intervals and temperatures will reach 13 degrees. AT the of Ireland there will be stormy weather temperatures will reach 7 degrees. In the midle of Ireland there will

Designs for a newspaper forecast.

Extension activity

- Maps for television weather forecasts are computer-generated. Some children could include a computer display as part of their presentation, for instance showing a graph of temperatures for the following day.

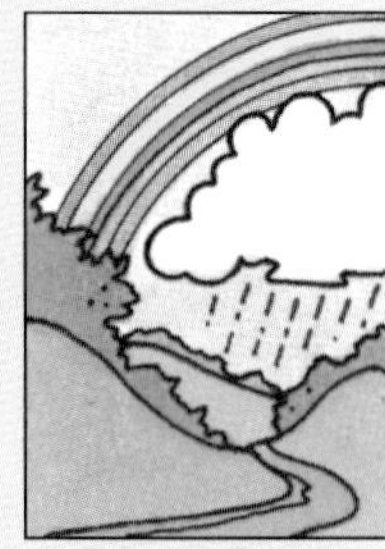

Weather

Seasons

The seasons are the result of the earth's orbit around the sun. They are the subject of some of the earliest examples of scientific, technological and artistic communication. For example, Stonehenge is said to be a form of 'observatory' for calculating solstices. A study of the seasons can lead to the children producing a range of writing.

Aims

- To develop skills of research and communicating information.

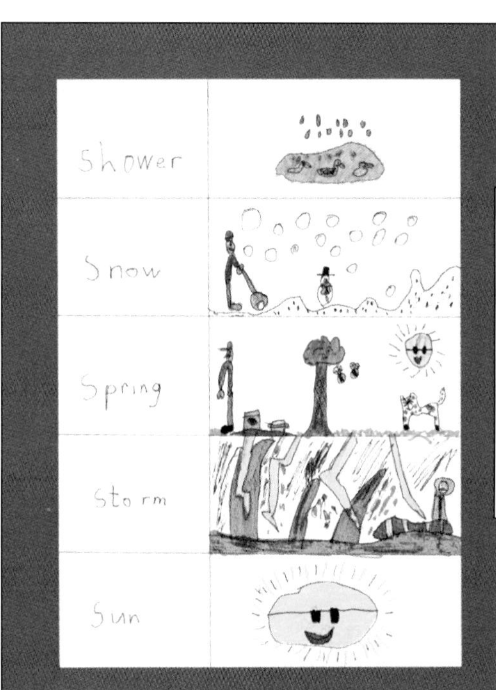

This child wrote and illustrated a book of words about the seasons. It was then used by the whole class as a reference book when writing about the weather and the seasons.

1 Preparation

- Plan a study of the seasons that is appropriate to the age range of the children. This might include observation and discussion of:
  - seasonal changes
  - the changing length of the day, including terms such as 'solstice' and 'equinox'
  - the earth's orbit around the sun
  - the different tasks in a farmer's year
  - seasonal changes to plants
  - behavioural patterns of animals through the year.

- The children should also experience some creative responses to the seasons, such as Vivaldi's *Four Seasons* and Thwaite's 'A Haiku Yearbook'.

Another child produced an illustrated chart to show the stages of the life of a hedgehog through the year.

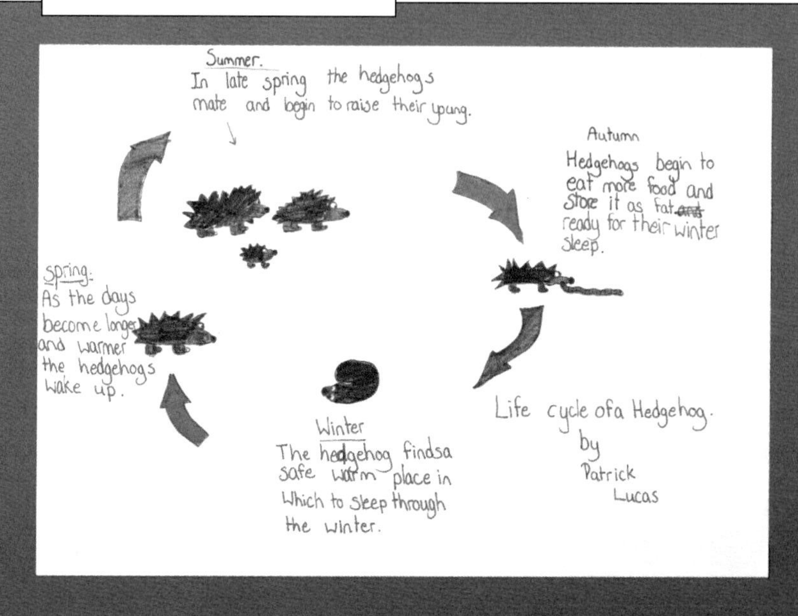

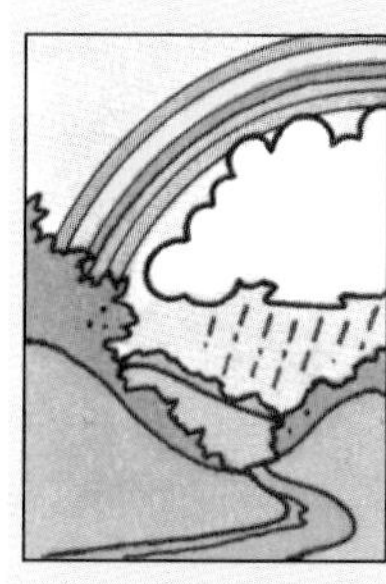

2 Observational posters and diaries

- The children could keep a diary over a period of change, for example from winter to spring. This should include information on the weather, the clothes people wear, the animals and birds that are seen and any other relevant information. They could record this information in the form of a large classroom poster.

A seasonal display.

3 Diagrams

- The children could research the annual cycle of a particular topic, such as farming, sports or animal behaviour. They could present their findings in the form of a circular diagram. Alternatively, they could describe their own annual cycle – birthdays, holidays, school and so on.

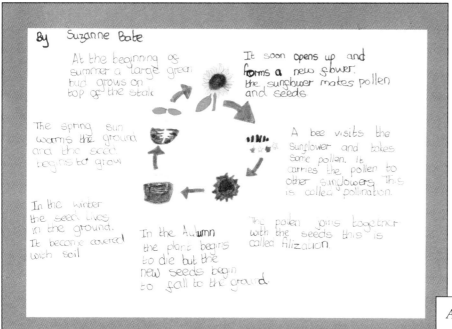

A seasonal calendar.

4 Information technology

- The children could experiment with computer-based diaries and electronic 'personal organisers', if these are available.

Extension activities

- Ask the children to find out about seasonal change in other parts of the world – where it is often very different – and to present the information they collect in a range of ways.
- A study of Stonehenge would make an exciting mini-topic. The children could research how the site may have been made and the beliefs that have been linked with it over the years.

Zoos

Organise a class debate on whether or not zoos are cruel to animals. Before the children express any opinions, they should find out as much as they can, so that their arguments are based on evidence. They should use library facilities for research, write to zoos for information and, if possible, visit a zoo for first-hand information.

Aims

To develop skills in:

- retrieving information
- expressing an opinion
- presenting a reasoned argument.

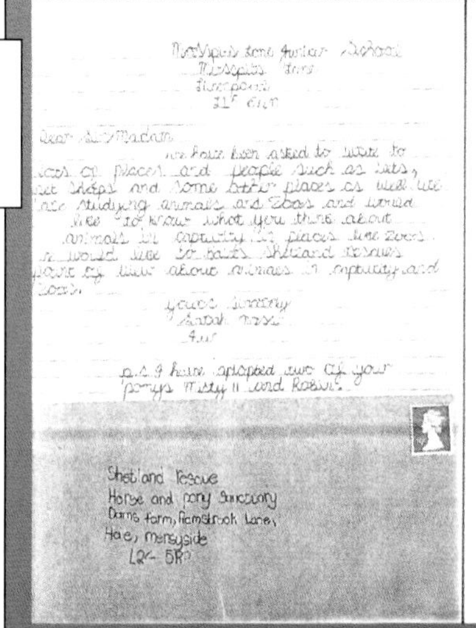

Dear Sir/Madam,

We have been asked to write to lots of places and people such as vets, pet shops and some other places as well. We are studying animals and zoos and would like to know what you think about animals in captivity in places like zoos. I would like to have Shetland Rescue's point of view about animals in captivity and zoos.

Yours sincerely

P.S. I have adopted two of your ponys ... and Robin.

Shetland Rescue
Horse and pony Sanctuary
Dams farm, Ramsbrook Lane,
Hale, Merseyside

SHETLAND RESCUE
HORSE & PONY SANCTUARY

The children wrote letters to request information from zoos and animal welfare groups.

1 Preparation

- Ask the children to write letters to zoos and animal welfare groups to collect as much information as they can about:
  - different kinds of zoo, animal enclosures, the keeper's job, feeding, breeding and so on
  - endangered animals such as pandas, gorillas, lemurs, African elephants, caimans and tigers
  - how zoos help to save endangered animals, for example the bison, the golden lion, the tamarin and the oryx
  - the ways in which animals are thought to suffer in captivity.

ZOO SURVEY

ZOOS CRUEL?	Votes
A YES	14
B DON'T KNOW	1
C NO	4

Harry found that most people thought that zoos are cruel.

ZOO SURVEY

ZOOS CRUEL?	Votes
A YES	14
B DON'T KNOW	1
C NO	4

From my survey I found that most people think zoos are cruel and only a few people think they are not.

Harry Gibbs 4W

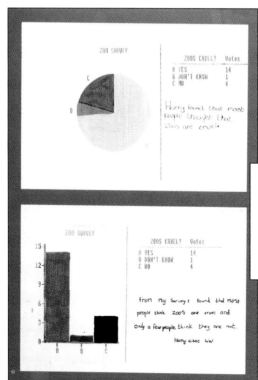

Harry surveyed people's opinions about zoos. The findings were presented in various ways.

2 Research

- Working in groups of four to six, the children could compile survey sheets to find out how other people feel about zoos.

3 Discussion

- The children could then hold a debate on the issue and end with a vote.

4 Preparation

- Having collected all the information and opinions, the children could present their findings in a variety of ways.
  - They could choose a point of view and plan a poster campaign to promote it. For example, they could feature pictures of suffering animals or contented animals.

The children designed posters showing different points of view.

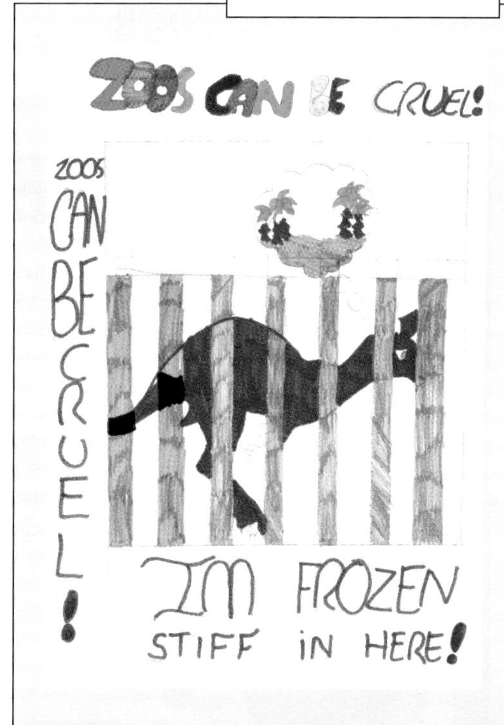

  - They could write and illustrate articles for newspapers or magazines giving information about their findings.
  - They could plan a documentary for a television programme and use a video camera to shoot some scenes.
  - Some children might like to produce some creative writing, imagining themselves to be the animals in question.

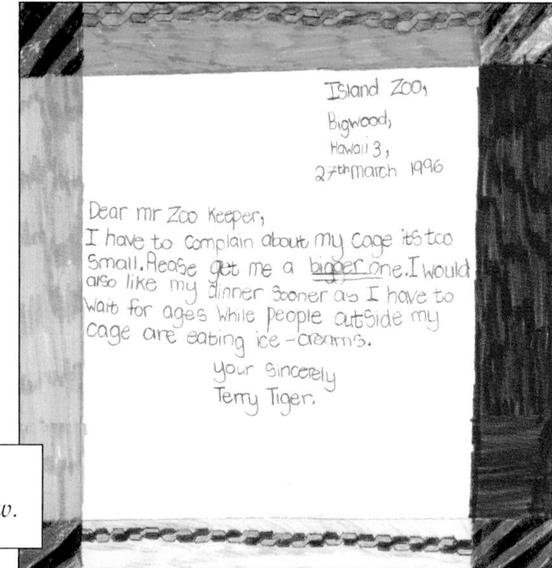

Island Zoo,
Bigwood,
Hawaii 3,
27th march 1996

Dear mr Zoo Keeper,
I have to complain about my cage its too Small. Please get me a bigger one. I would also like my dinner Sooner as I have to wait for ages while people outside my cage are eating ice-creams.

your Sincerely
Terry Tiger.

One child wrote a letter from a tigers point of view.

Extension activities

- The children could find out about, and express opinions on:
  - the tactics used by animal rights organisations
  - the ivory trade
  - game reserves in Africa
  - deforestation and its effects on wildlife.

Pets

Aims

To develop skills in writing:

- precise instructions
- clear descriptions.

Pets make an ideal focus for writing about animals, as many children have a pet or would like to have one. In particular, the children should think and write about the animals' needs. This involves careful research, planning and writing precise instructions and accurate descriptions.

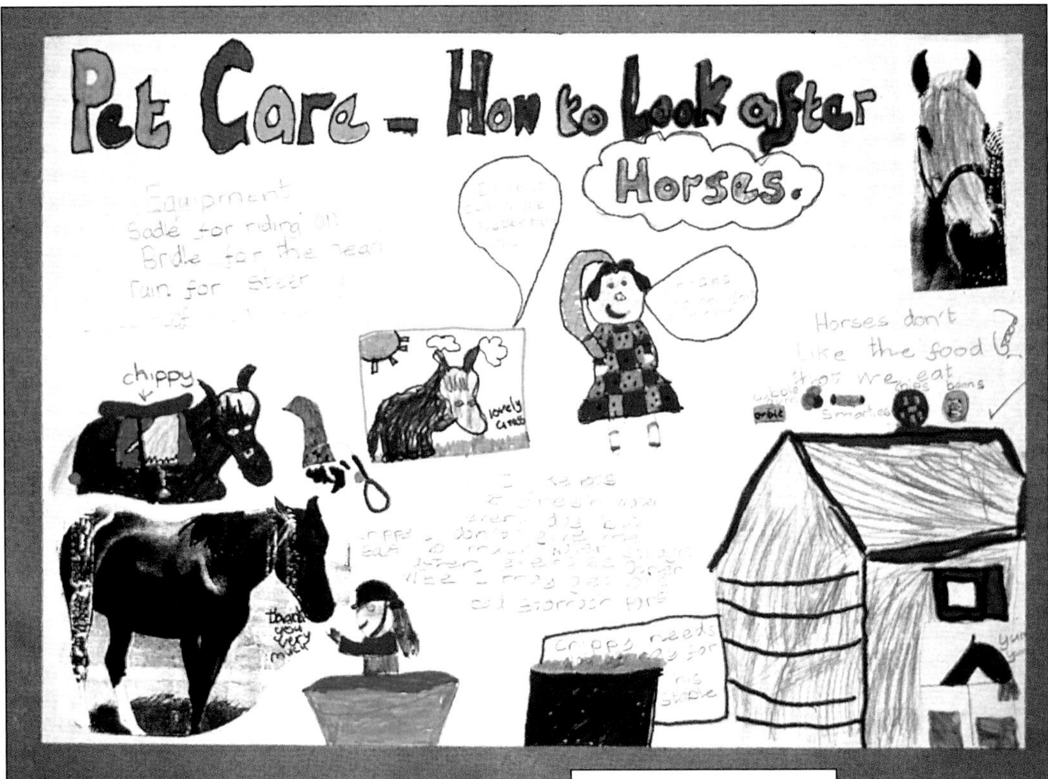

One group of children chose to study horses.

1 Preparation

- Discuss the different pets that people own and how and where they are kept.
- Divide the children into groups. Each group is to write an instruction pack on how to look after a particular type of pet. The pack can include a booklet, a poster and a list of DOS and DON'TS.
- Each group should list questions to be answered, using the school's and local libraries.

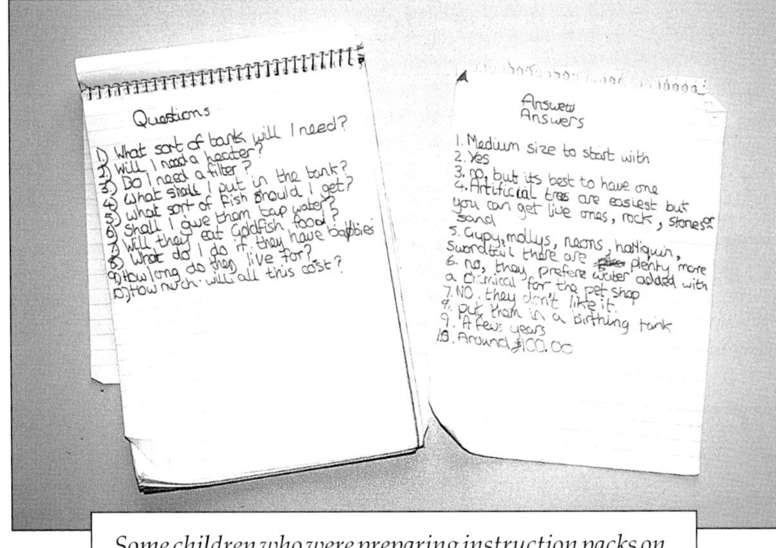

Some children who were preparing instruction packs on tropical fish made this list of subjects to research.

2 Presentation

- The children should discuss their findings and decide how to present their information clearly and effectively. The work can be divided among group members.

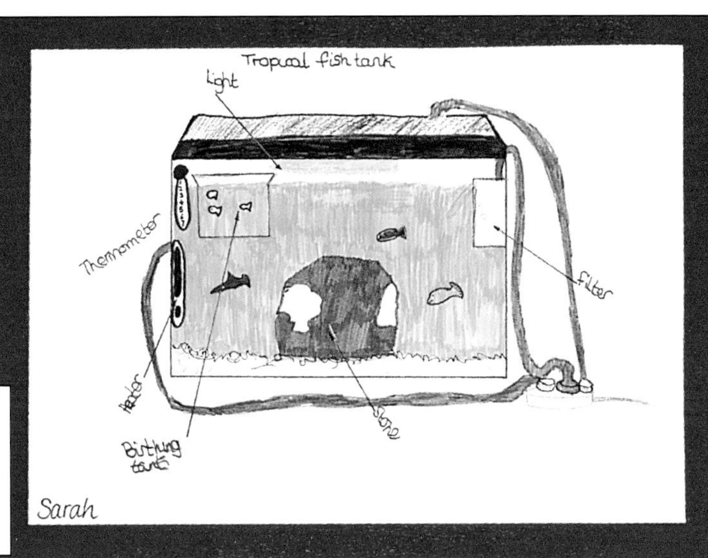

An annotated drawing of a fish tank shows clearly the environment that tropical fish need.

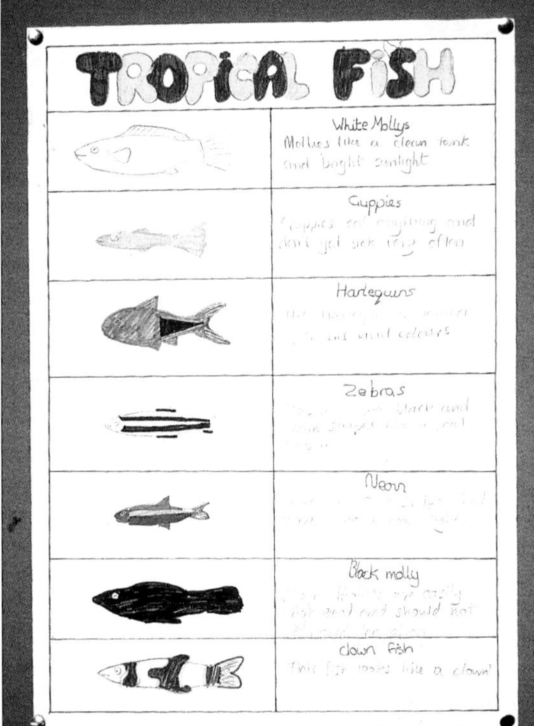

An informative poster.

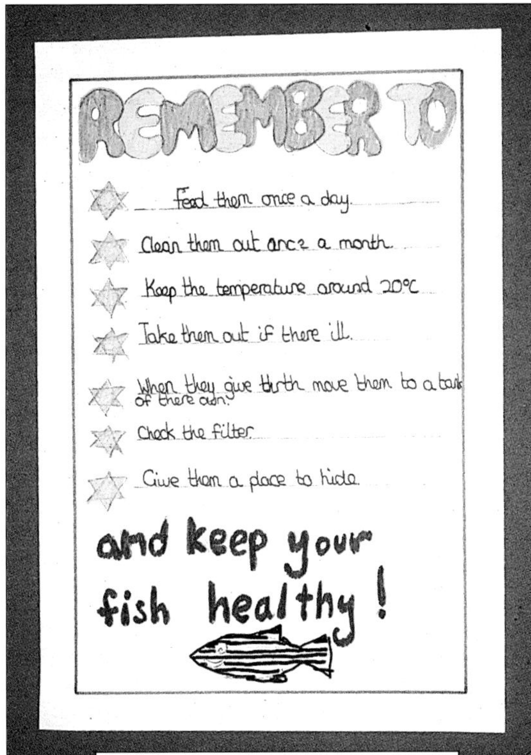

An instructive poster, designed to be displayed above a fish tank.

3 Information technology

- The children could create a database of information about favourite pets, their habits and needs.

Extension activity

- Each group could give an oral presentation of the information that has been collected. They should plan and prepare visual aids, such as a list of points on an acetate sheet for an overhead projector, computer displays or a video of pets at home.

Animals

Habitats

Another interesting aspect of animals is their habitat. A science project studying animals' adaptation to habitats and the feeding relationships within habitats provides an opportunity for children to develop the skill of presenting information through words and pictures.

Aims

To develop skills in:

- accurate observation and note-taking
- presenting information in graphic form
- combining graphic information with text in an effective way.

One group produced notes and sketches on a hedgerow habitat.

1 Preparation

- Choose a habitat for the children to study, such as a garden, hedgerow, woodland or pond. Let them observe it for a period of time, during which they should make notes and sketches, including:
  - a description of the habitat, mentioning the animals and plants that live there
  - comments on how the animals have adapted to their habitat, for example the food they eat and the camouflage they use
  - a sketch of the habitat, showing the animals' movements in it.
- The children will need to support their observations with library research.

The group then went on to make an illustated plan of a woodland habitat that showed the movements of a rabbit they observed there.

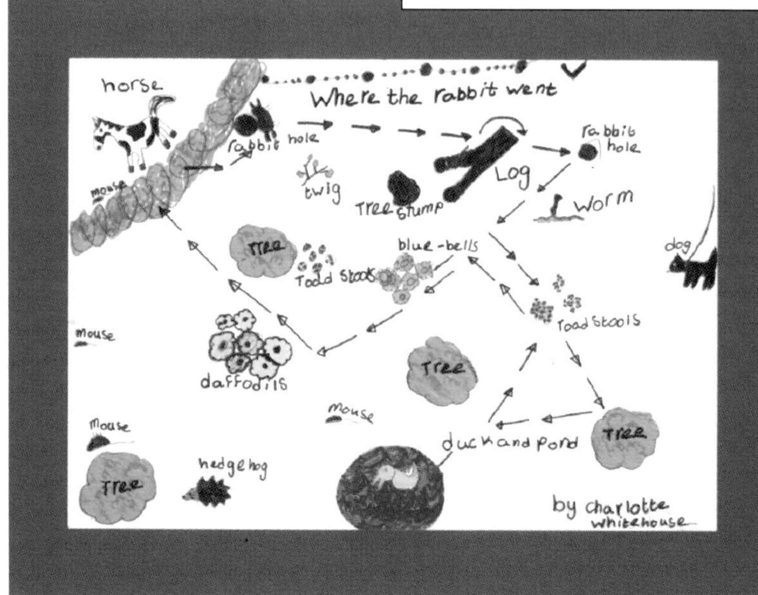

2 Presenting the information

- The children could review the material that they have researched and consider how to present it. For example, as a chapter for an illustrated reference book or as an educational poster.
- Different types of illustrations and text should be combined in an interesting way. The children could look at publishers' reference books and posters for ideas on how to do this.

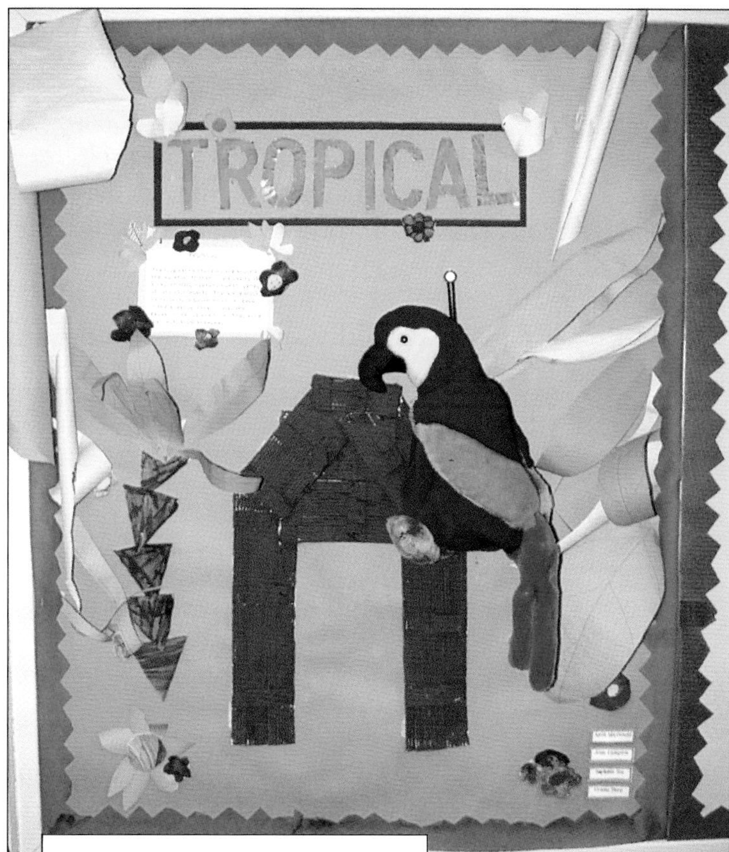

Two groups investigated different habitats and then, using computer print-outs of their research, produced posters about the habitats and their inhabitants.

Extension activity

- The children could plan a habitat in the school grounds. This would enable them to study animals on a daily basis without having to travel too far. They could keep notebooks on the activities within their habitat over a long period of time.

Transport

A traffic survey

The increasing amount of traffic on roads is an important environmental issue. It should be possible to let the children investigate the issue by focusing on a particular local road junction. They could present their findings and decide whether the road layout needs changing or whether traffic-calming measures need to be introduced. Plan visits to such places carefully and give the children clear safety instructions.

Aims

To develop skills of:

- accurate observation and recording of data
- analysing data
- presenting data in a clear and interesting way.

1 Preparation

- Divide the class into groups to study a busy road junction for a certain length of time. Give each child a specific task. The tasks could include:
  - counting the cars, buses, vans and lorries that use the junction
  - counting the vehicles travelling in each direction
  - collecting information on the commercial traffic, such as the names of the companies that own the vehicles, the places they come from (if written on the side of the vehicles), and so on
  - drawing the junction and making notes about the road signs and markings
  - noting the provision for pedestrians and estimating their numbers at certain times of the day
  - seeking the opinion of regular road and pavement users at the junction to find out whether they feel changes are needed.

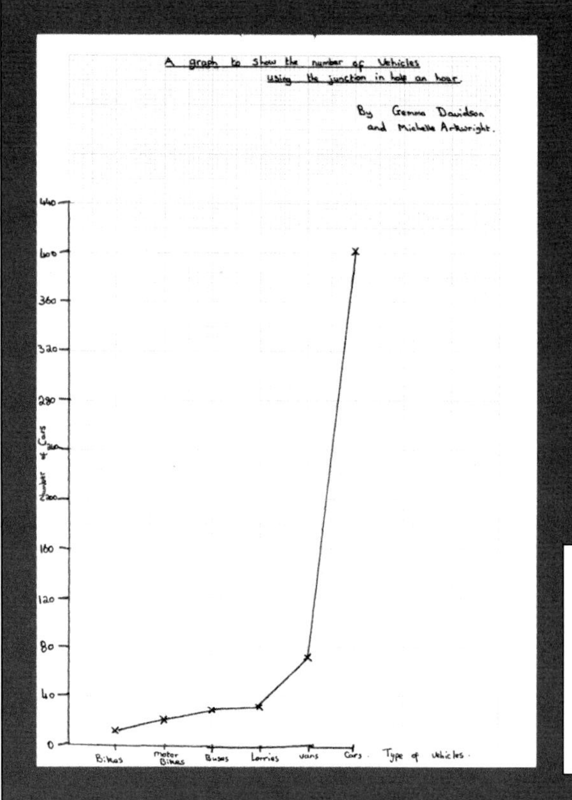

Some of the information could be presented in the form of a graph.

The children could make sketches and plans of the road layout to refer to later.

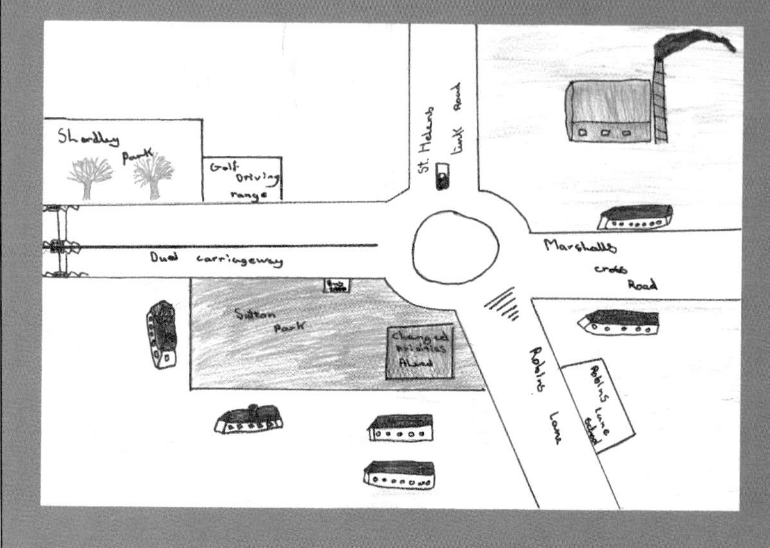

2 Drawing conclusions

- Having completed the field study, the children could present their findings and suggest improvements or solutions, such as:
  - there are too many heavy goods vehicles – a bypass is needed
  - vehicles are travelling too fast – traffic-calming measures are needed
  - pedestrians cannot cross – a pelican crossing is needed.

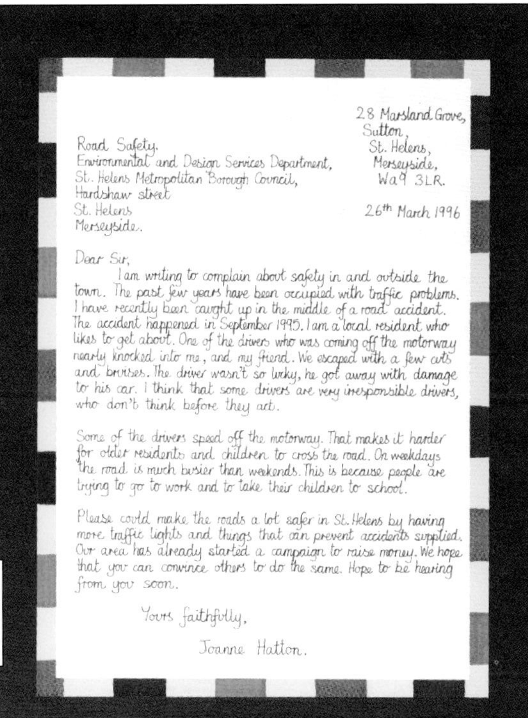

28 Marsland Grove,
Sutton,
St. Helens,
Merseyside,
Wa9 3LR.

Road Safety.
Environmental and Design Services Department,
St. Helens Metropolitan Borough Council,
Hardshaw street
St. Helens
Merseyside.

26th March 1996

Dear Sir,

I am writing to complain about safety in and outside the town. The past few years have been occupied with traffic problems. I have recently been caught up in the middle of a road accident. The accident happened in September 1995. I am a local resident who likes to get about. One of the drivers who was coming off the motorway nearly knocked into me, and my friend. We escaped with a few cuts and bruises. The driver wasn't so lucky, he got away with damage to his car. I think that some drivers are very irresponsible drivers, who don't think before they act.

Some of the drivers speed off the motorway. That makes it harder for older residents and children to cross the road. On weekdays the road is much busier than weekends. This is because people are trying to go to work and to take their children to school.

Please could make the roads a lot safer in St. Helens by having more traffic lights and things that can prevent accidents supplied. Our area has already started a campaign to raise money. We hope that you can convince others to do the same. Hope to be hearing from you soon.

Yours faithfully,

Joanne Hatton.

Letters and recorded comments from road users.

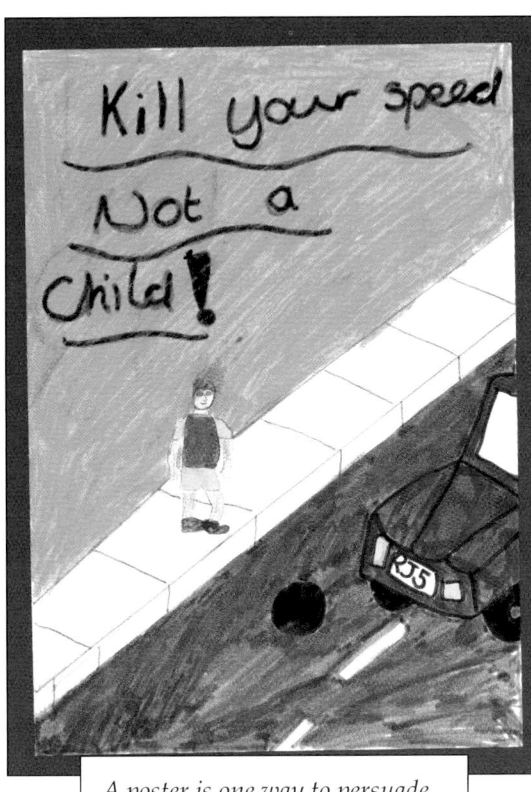

A poster is one way to persuade.

3 Presentation

- The children could plan to present their findings and suggestions for improvements to the local authority. They should have the evidence available in a variety of forms, such as:
  - statistics presented on an overhead projector
  - a poster that raises awareness
  - a leaflet that lists the findings and conclusions
  - plans for a bypass or traffic-calming measures
  - a display of comments obtained from pedestrians and drivers who use the junction.

Extension activities

- The data collected by the children might suggest several additional activities, such as:
  - redesigning the junction
  - adding pedestrian safety features
  - designing posters to encourage the use of public transport and car-sharing.

Bypass

The activity here is designed to stimulate a debate about the need for a bypass around a town or village. The children need to investigate the reasons for constructing a bypass and examine the different points of view that can be apparent when a bypass is proposed. It might be possible to link this work with the study of a road junction as suggested on pages 48–49. Otherwise, an example of a bypass scheme currently in the news or an imaginary bypass scheme could be used as the subject.

Aims

To develop skills of:

- persuasion, using a variety of forms and media
- interviewing and reporting.

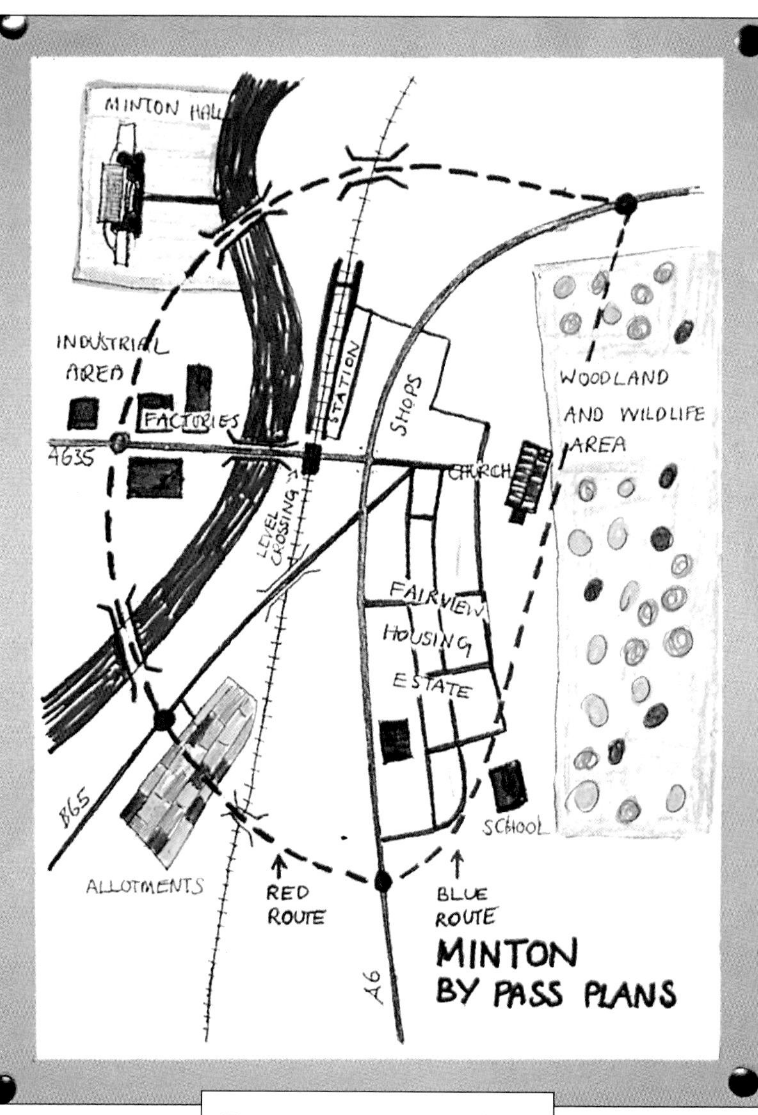

Two routes were proposed for a bypass around Minton.

1 Preparation

- Explain to the children that they are going to plan a campaign to persuade others of their opinion. Divide them into the following groups and ask them to study a map of the town showing the proposed routes for the bypass:
  - a residents' committee that will speak up for the interests of the people who live in the town
  - an environmentalists' pressure group that will defend open spaces, wildlife habitats and so on
  - farmers, whose land is to be cut across
  - business people and shopkeepers who fear that the bypass will cause people to shop elsewhere
  - a news team to interview the different groups and write reports for the local papers.

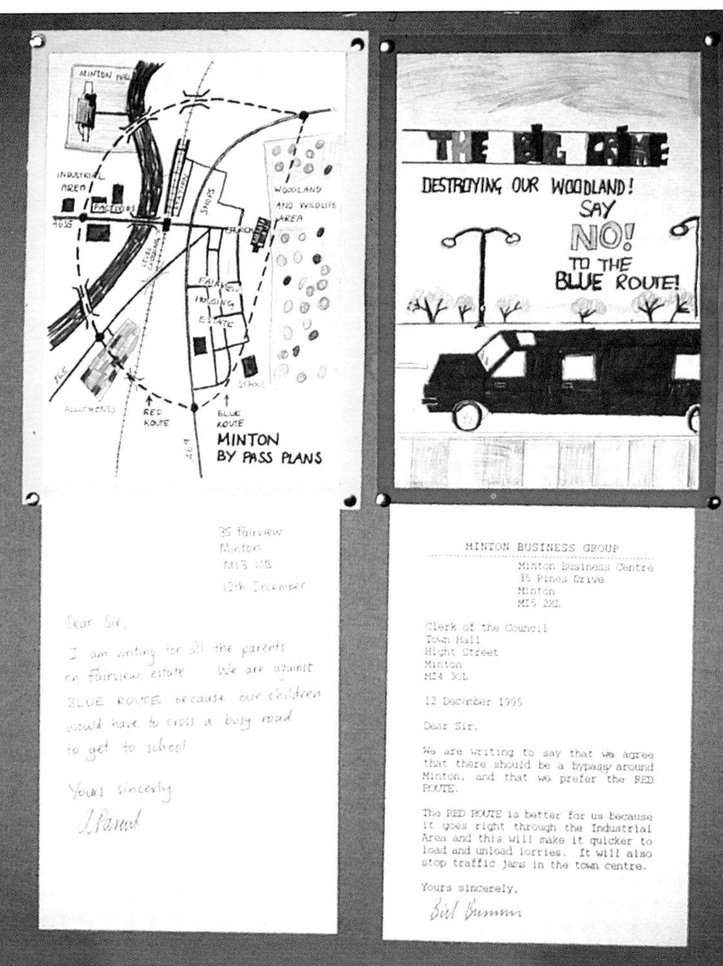

Different interest groups produced posters and letters expressing their points of view.

Transport

2 The campaign

- Each group (except for the news team) should produce letters, posters and so on, for its campaign. These could all be combined in one large class display.
- After a class discussion, a vote could be taken on the best route for the bypass.

3 Recording

- While the various pressure groups are investigating and presenting their information, the news team should interview them, take (or draw) pictures and present a newspaper front page using information technology.

Extension activity

- One representative from each group could join a committee of enquiry chaired by the class teacher. After the presentation of all the evidence and points of view, the committee could make a decision about the bypass.

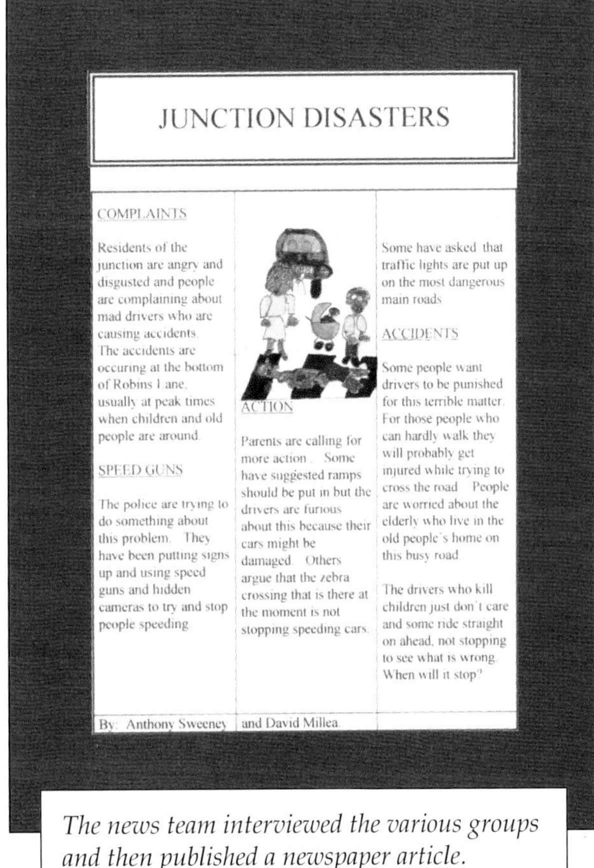

JUNCTION DISASTERS

COMPLAINTS

Residents of the junction are angry and disgusted and people are complaining about mad drivers who are causing accidents. The accidents are occuring at the bottom of Robins Lane, usually at peak times when children and old people are around.

SPEED GUNS

The police are trying to do something about this problem. They have been putting signs up and using speed guns and hidden cameras to try and stop people speeding.

ACTION

Parents are calling for more action. Some have suggested ramps should be put in but the drivers are furious about this because their cars might be damaged. Others argue that the zebra crossing that is there at the moment is not stopping speeding cars.

Some have asked that traffic lights are put up on the most dangerous main roads.

ACCIDENTS

Some people want drivers to be punished for this terrible matter. For those people who can hardly walk they will probably get injured while trying to cross the road. People are worried about the elderly who live in the old people's home on this busy road.

The drivers who kill children just don't care and some ride straight on ahead, not stopping to see what is wrong. When will it stop?

By: Anthony Sweeney and David Millea.

The news team interviewed the various groups and then published a newspaper article.

Journeys

There is a lot of debate on the damage to the environment from the number of cars using the roads. There is also concern about the number of accidents on the roads. There is a campaign to persuade people to leave their cars at home and to use public transport. The children could use this debate to undertake some interesting writing.

Aims
To develop skills of:
- planning
- personal writing.

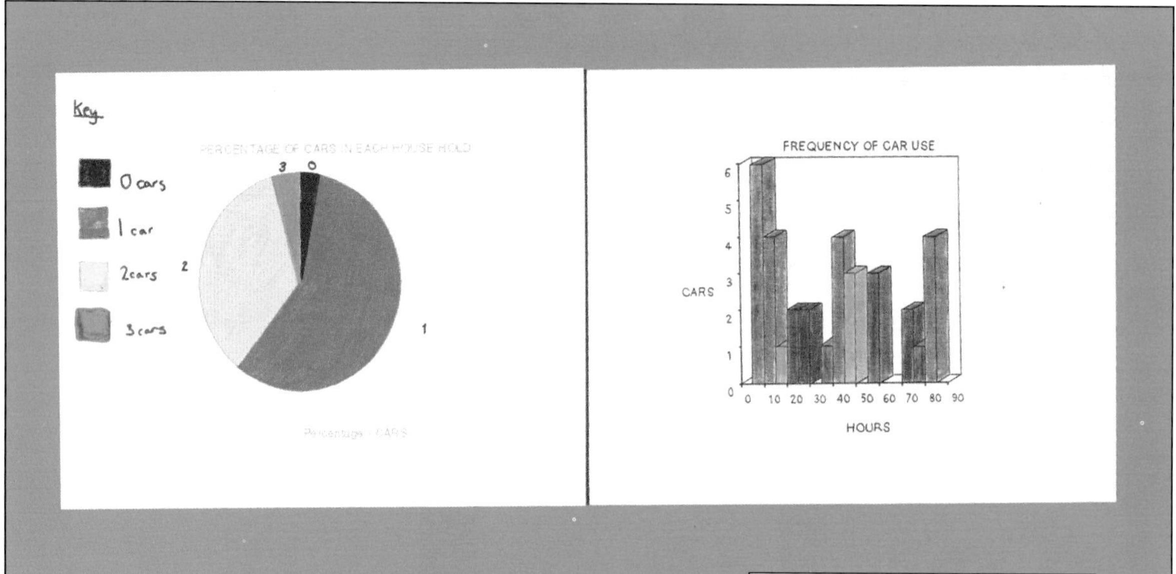

The children surveyed the number of cars owned by families in the school and the number of hours per week that they were used.

1 Preparation

- Ask the children to undertake a variety of surveys both in the school and at home. These could address:
  – the number of cars owned by the children's families
  – the different ways in which the children travel to and from school
  – the purposes for which the families' cars are used, such as travelling to work, visiting relatives, going shopping, leisure
  – the number of accidents that have occurred in the locality.

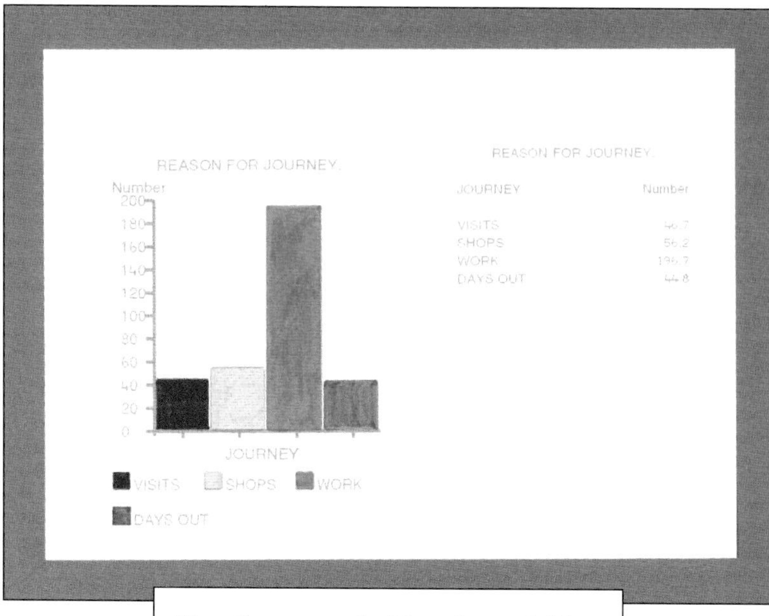

They then researched for what activities the cars were used and how often.

2 Research

- The children could write to different organisations to try to establish:
  - how much pollution is caused by traffic
  - how many accidents have occurred locally
  - what public transport there is, its frequency, area of coverage and reliability.

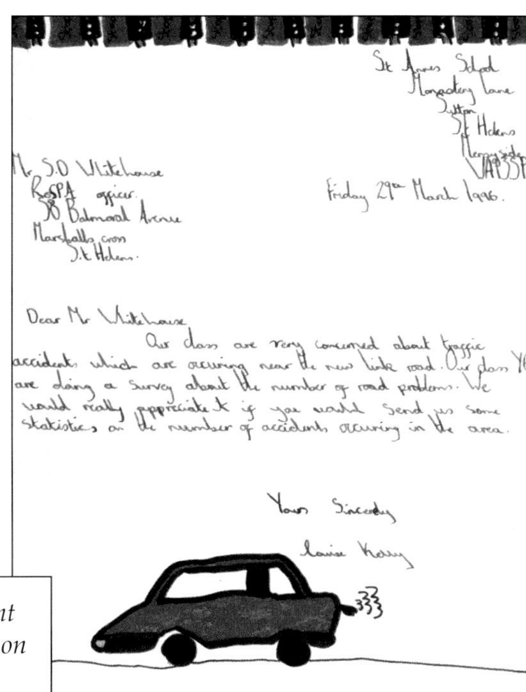

St Annes School
Mongosley Lane
Sutton
St Helens
Merseyside
WA9 3SP

Mr. S.O Whitehouse
RoSPA officer.
38 Balmoral Avenue
Marshalls cross
St Helens.

Friday 29th March 1996.

Dear Mr Whitehouse

Our class are very concerned about traffic accidents which are occuring near the new link road. Our class Y6 are doing a survey about the number of road problems. We would really appreciate it if you would send us some statistics on the number of accidents occuring in the area.

Yours Sincerely

Louise Kavy

One group wrote letters to different organisations asking for statistics on accidents and pollution.

3 The campaign

- The campaign is to persuade people to use their cars less and public transport more. To do this, the children will need to bring the facts to the attention of local residents. This can be done by:
  - designing informative posters
  - printing leaflets
  - writing letters and articles for the local newspaper
  - holding debates at school to which parents and friends are invited.

USE A BIKE

NOT A CAR

Finally, the children undertook a poster campaign to persuade people to use their cars less.

Extension activity

- Plan a campaign to persuade people to walk more. Let the children find out how fit they are and how used they are to walking. How quickly do they get out of breath? How many miles do they walk each week?

Inventors and inventions

This is a good subject for a cross-curricular topic, allowing the children to cover aspects of history, science, technology and art. At the same time they can practise a range of different types of writing.

Aims

- To develop reference and research skills.
- To provide experience of the biographical style of writing.

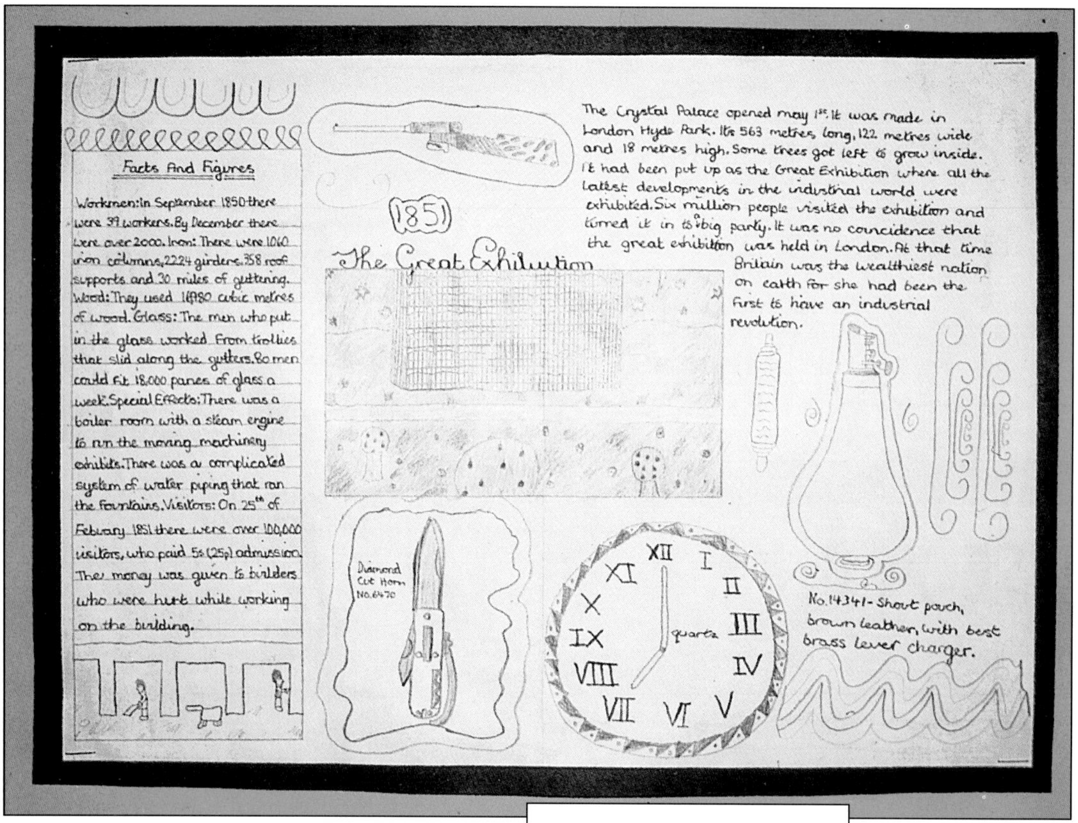

The Great Exhibition was used as the focus for work on inventions. This work was linked with a broader study of the Victorians.

1 Preparation

- Ensure that the necessary books are available in the school library. Different categories of non-fiction will need to be clearly labelled. If the Dewey system is used, make sure that the children understand it. It is a good idea to set up a reference-only section containing general reference works, encyclopaedias, and a multi-media PC (if funds allow).

2 Research

- The children should work in pairs to research an individual inventor or the development of a particular invention.
- They should make a list of questions to investigate, before going to the library.
- Encourage them to note down key facts only, not to copy out whole chunks of text from the books that they consult.

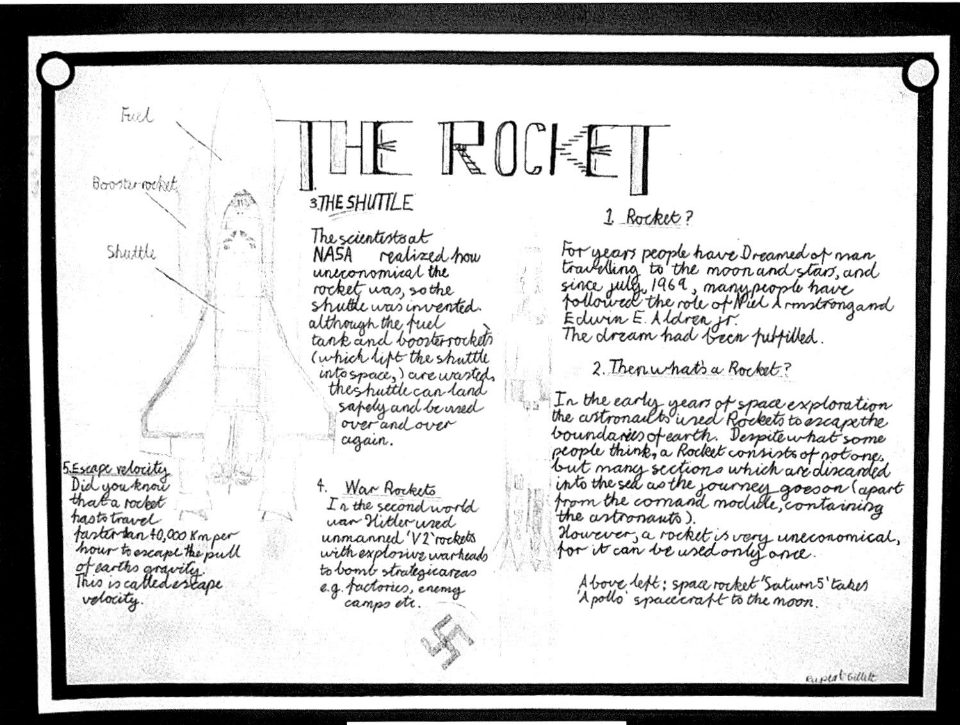

THE ROCKET
Fuel
Booster rocket
Shuttle
3. THE SHUTTLE
The scientists at NASA realized how uneconomical the rocket was, so the shuttle was invented. although the fuel tank and booster rockets (which lift the shuttle into space,) are wasted, the shuttle can land safely and be used over and over again.
1. Rocket?
For years people have Dreamed of man travelling to the moon and stars, and since july, 1969, many people have followed the role of Neil Armstrong and Edwin E. Aldrea jr. The dream had been fulfilled.
2. Then what's a Rocket?
In the early years of space exploration the astronauts used Rockets to escape the boundaries of earth. Despite what some people think, a Rocket consists of not one, but many sections which are discarded into the sea as the journey goes on (apart from the command module, containing the astronauts).
However, a rocket is very uneconomical, for it can be used only once.
Above left: space rocket 'Saturn 5' takes 'Apollo' spacecraft to the moon.
5. Escape velocity
Did you know that a rocket has to travel faster than 40,000 Km per hour to escape the pull of earths gravity. This is called escape velocity.
4. War Rockets
In the second world war Hitler used unmanned 'V2' rockets with explosive warheads to bomb strategic areas e.g. factories, enemy camps etc.

One child decided to research the invention of the space shuttle.

3 A biography

- The children could bring their notes together in the form of a biography, which is a factual account of a person's life and work. Ask them to think of their own age group as the audience for the biography. This will prevent them from copying out passages from reference books, as they will need to write in simpler language. A good biography will contain:
  - 'human interest', such as early struggles, problems at school, triumph over difficulties
  - a clear framework of dates and key facts.

4 Information technology

- Set up a class database of inventors.
- Ask pairs of children to prepare a summary of their biography. Discuss and agree a format (word limit, inclusion of key dates and so on) for all the summaries.
- End with a database quiz that will require all the children to interrogate the class database.

Extension activities

- Present the information researched in different formats:
  - a newspaper article announcing a new invention
  - an imaginary diary written by an inventor
  - the inventor's biography written in story form
  - a storyboard version of the biography.

Inventions

Making and marketing

Having investigated past inventors and inventions, the children could go on to design and make their own invention. This provides opportunities for several kinds of writing.

Aims

- To explore a range of writing related to the making of a product.
- To develop practical skills of planning and designing.
- To practise taking notes when gathering information.

1 Preparation

- Organise the children into small groups and ask them to decide what product they intend to 'invent'.

2 Market research

- The children should observe and research the views of other children, teachers and parents about their intended invention. For example:
  - do they already have an example of this particular item?
  - could it be improved in any way?
- They should analyse their findings and list the main features that need to be incorporated into their invention.

The children made sketches showing their designs for a desk-tidy container.

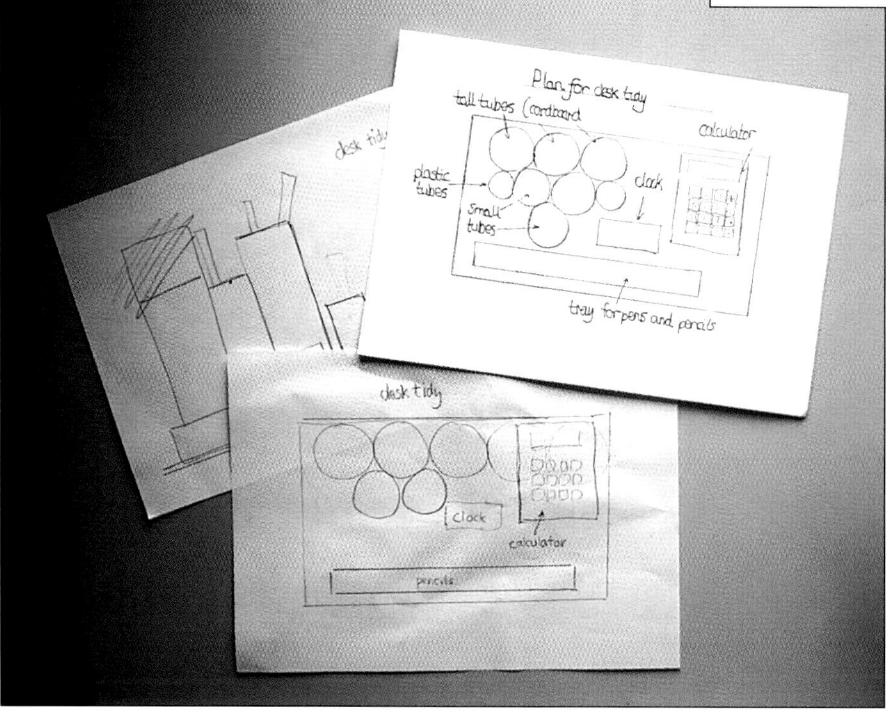

3 Designing

- Taking into account the results of their market research, the children could make annotated sketches showing the design of their invention.
- They could list all the materials required to make it.
- They could modify their plans if necessary, for example if the material they need is not available they should investigate others.

4 The final product

- Let the children get together all the materials that they need to make their final product.

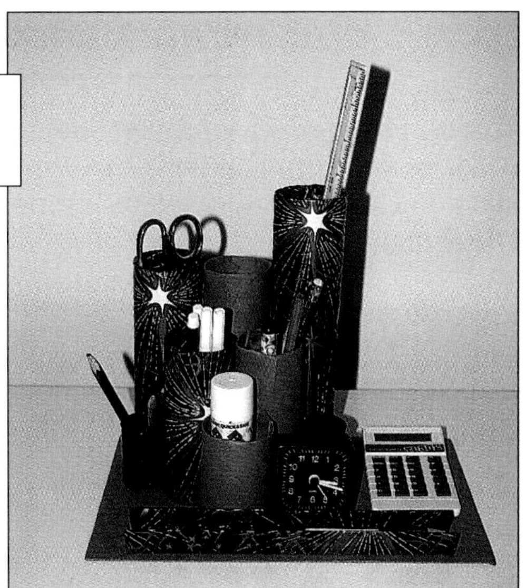

The final product: a desk-tidy container

5 Packaging

- It is often the packaging that persuades the purchaser that he or she needs a product. Ask the children to think about the type of packaging that their product needs. They should create a company logo and a slogan for their product.

Inventions

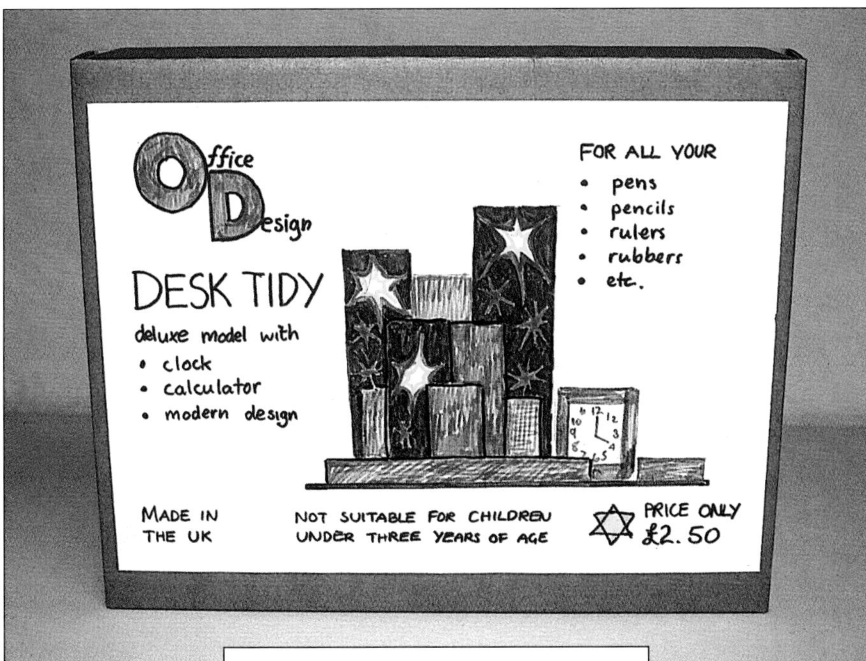

The advertising campaign was carefully planned and was supported by some lively posters.

6 An advertising campaign

- Ask the children to plan a large campaign to sell their product. The campaign should include featuring the product in newspapers, in magazines, on the radio and on television.

They will need to think about:
- how long the campaign should last
- which newspapers and magazines would be the best to advertise in
- the design and size of the advertisement
- the difference between a radio and a television advertisement
- what is actually said or shown during the advertisement.

Vikings

Using research

This chapter shows how different types of writing can be used not only to enhance the acquisition of historical skills and knowledge but also to enhance the development of writing required for English and for research skills.

Aims

To develop the skills of:

- research
- representing information in a creative way
- writing in a range of forms.

1 Preparation

- Bring a range of good quality reference materials to the classroom, if possible leaving some key reference works (including a CD-ROM, if available) in the library, so that the opportunity can be taken to develop library research.

2 Task allocation

- Divide the class into groups to research the following topics:
  - Where did the Vikings come from?
  - What were their language and writing like?
  - Which places did they capture?
  - Describe one particular raid in detail.
  - What kind of clothes did they wear?
  - How did the Anglo-Saxons fight back?
  - Which other parts of the world did they visit?
  - What were their ships like?

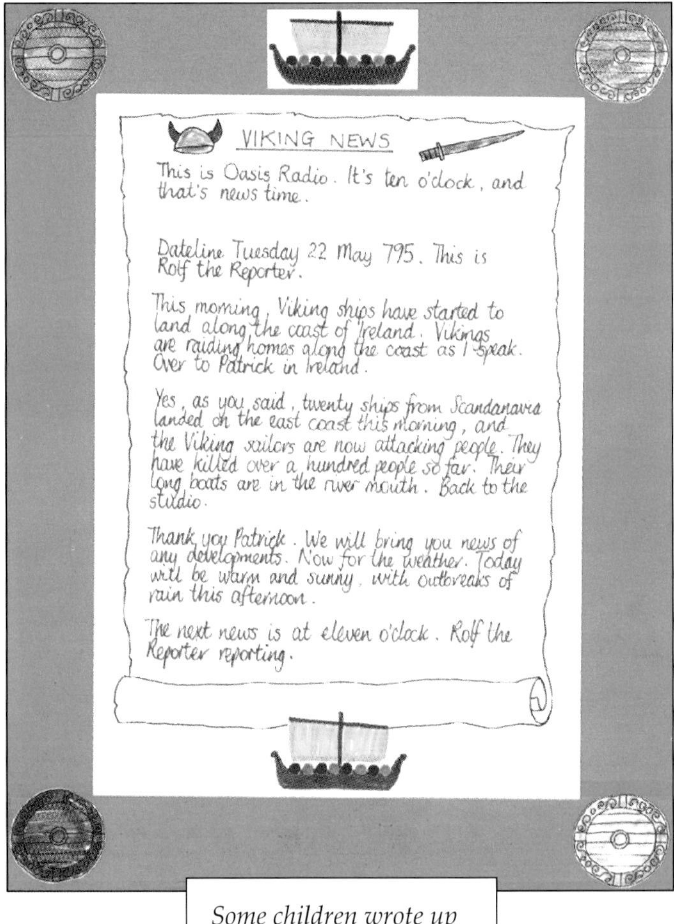

VIKING NEWS

This is Oasis Radio. It's ten o'clock, and that's news time.

Dateline Tuesday 22 May 795. This is Rolf the Reporter.

This morning, Viking ships have started to land along the coast of Ireland. Vikings are raiding homes along the coast as I speak. Over to Patrick in Ireland.

Yes, as you said, twenty ships from Scandanavia landed on the east coast this morning, and the Viking sailors are now attacking people. They have killed over a hundred people so far. Their long boats are in the river mouth. Back to the studio.

Thank you Patrick. We will bring you news of any developments. Now for the weather. Today will be warm and sunny, with outbreaks of rain this afternoon.

The next news is at eleven o'clock. Rolf the Reporter reporting.

Some children wrote up their research in the form of a news bulletin.

3 Writing up the research

- The best way to help children avoid copying out whole chunks of their source material is to suggest that they present their research in different forms, some examples of which are shown on these pages. For example:
  - pictures and diagrams
  - diaries
  - news bulletins
  - word games.

- News bulletins can capture the language and style of modern news broadcasts – no hint of copying from resource material here!
- A diary is a very useful format for writing a detailed account of an historical event, but without the danger of copying out.
- Wordfinders, wordsearches or crossword puzzles represent research information in a creative and interesting way. Often this type of activity can help children to learn basic facts more quickly than than the conventional essay.

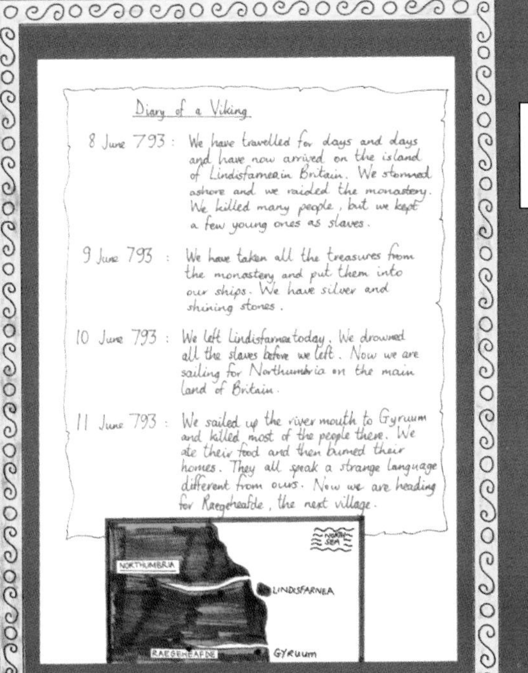

Diary of a Viking

8 June 793: We have travelled for days and days and have now arrived on the island of Lindisfarnein Britain. We stormed ashore and we raided the monastery. We killed many people, but we kept a few young ones as slaves.

9 June 793: We have taken all the treasures from the monastery and put them into our ships. We have silver and shining stones.

10 June 793: We left Lindisfarne today. We drowned all the slaves before we left. Now we are sailing for Northumbria on the main land of Britain.

11 June 793: We sailed up the river mouth to Gyruum and killed most of the people there. We ate their food and then burned their homes. They all speak a strange language different from ours. Now we are heading for Raegeheafde, the next village.

This child captured the informal style of diary writing.

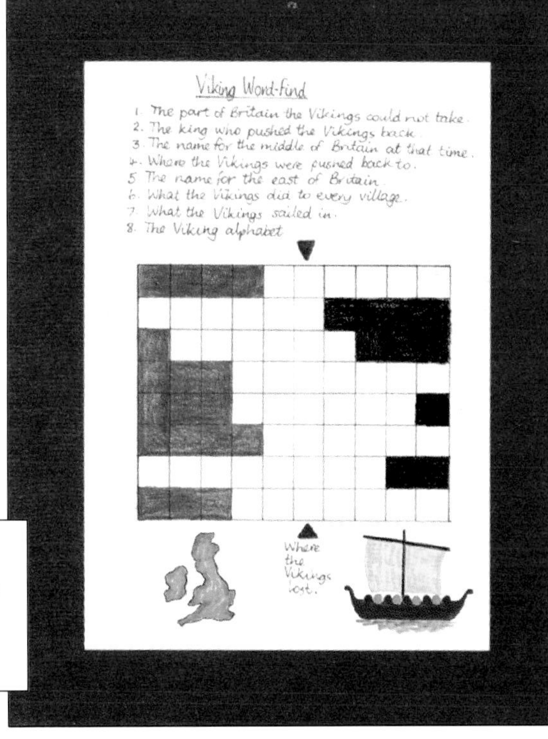

Viking Word-find

1. The part of Britain the Vikings could not take.
2. The king who pushed the Vikings back.
3. The name for the middle of Britain at that time.
4. Where the Vikings were pushed back to.
5. The name for the east of Britain.
6. What the Vikings did to every village.
7. What the Vikings sailed in.
8. The Viking alphabet.

As well as being fun to do, the wordfinder is a valuable method by which children learn facts.

Extension activities

- Here is a range of other forms that can be used to represent research information:
  - newspaper front page
  - story
  - poem
  - adventure game
  - storyboard
  - letter or postcard.

Vikings

Writing a reference book

A class reference book can be used with a wide range of topics, and is particularly suited to the humanities. The children could write their own reference book. This will involve them in a range of types of writing as well as provide them with the huge satisfaction of seeing the end result.

Aims

To develop skills of:

- writing non-fiction
- representing research information.

1 Preparation

- Tell the children that they are going to produce their own textbook on the Vikings, and that it will have all the key features of a good modern reference book. Explain that their audience will be next year's class, and that the purpose will be to help next year's class study the topic.

2 Research

- Groups of children should look carefully at the design and layout of other reference books that you have been using for the topic. Ask them to look for:
  - the use of different sizes and styles of type
  - page layout in boxes and columns
  - titles and subtitles
  - the use of charts, diagrams and pictures
  - contents page
  - index page
  - bullet points.

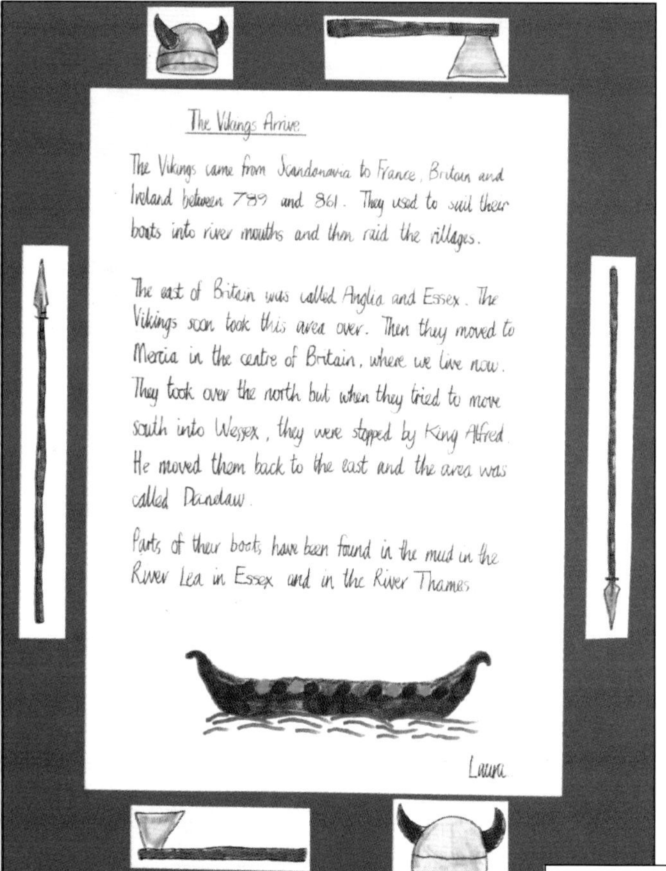

The Vikings Arrive

The Vikings came from Scandanavia to France, Britain and Ireland between 789 and 861. They used to sail their boats into river mouths and then raid the villages.

The east of Britain was called Anglia and Essex. The Vikings soon took this area over. Then they moved to Mercia in the centre of Britain, where we live now. They took over the north but when they tried to move south into Wessex, they were stopped by King Alfred He moved them back to the east and the area was called Danelaw.

Parts of their boats have been found in the mud in the River Lea in Essex and in the River Thames.

Laura

'The Vikings Arrive' is an historical account written from brief but relevant notes that contained keywords and important dates.

3 Task allocation

- Divide the class into groups of three or four. Ask each to produce a page for the book. They should research the topic and design an attractively laid out page using some of the features listed above. Types of writing for the book could include:
  - alphabet lists
  - word lists
  - reproduction of original sources
  - factual writing.
- To avoid children copying chunks of text, ask them to read the source material carefully and to make notes. These could be confined to dates and keywords to remind them of the order of events. The children could then write the historical account from their notes.

Vikings

- One group of children could explore Viking runes, and design an attractive page on the runic alphabet. This alphabet could then be used as a useful reference for writing phrases, poems, plaques for wall-displays and stories in runes.
- The children could research the places that the Vikings captured and organise the place names into alphabetical order. This could be colourfully illustrated with maps and pictures of battles and serve as a useful reference page to aid the writing of time lines, stories and word games.

One child designed a page on the runic alphabet.

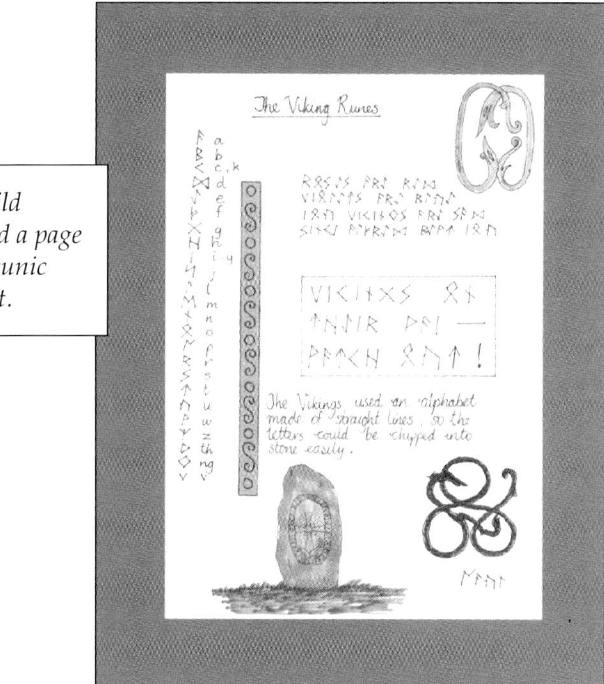

- The writing of a page of relevant words about Vikings (a Viking word bank) is a useful exercise in which the children can discover the key features of Viking times. The page could be organised into the columns: proper nouns, common nouns and verbs. This is a useful basis for various forms of writing, such as diaries, letters and poems.

Another child researched the places that the Vikings captured.

An Alphabet of Viking Captures
Anglia, Britain, Caithness, Danelaw, Essex, Flanders, Godmundingham, Humber, Ireland, Jutland, Kent, Lindisfarne, Mercia, Northumbria, Orkneys, Paris, Q, Russia, Scarborough, Thames, U, V, Wessex, X, York, Z

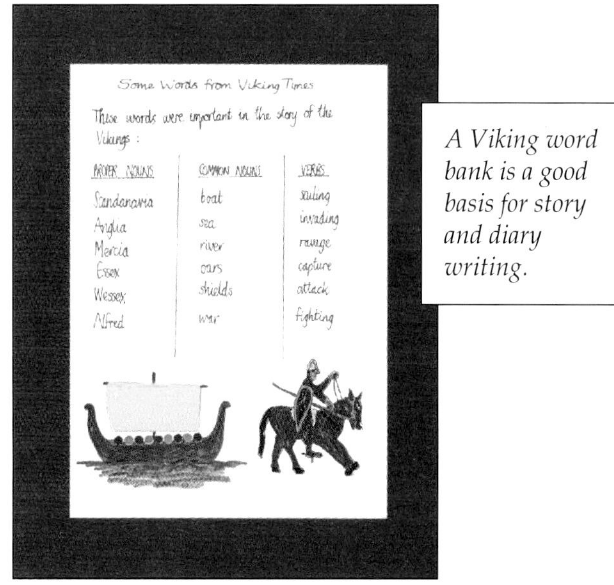

A Viking word bank is a good basis for story and diary writing.

Extension activities

- A cover could be designed for the book. You may wish to laminate this to give extra strength.
- Some children could write a contents and an index page for the book.

Copiable sheets

Topic planner

Topic: **Term:** **Week:**

Aims	Subject Attainment Targets	Cross-curricular links	Differentiation	Resources
Evaluation				

Assessment sheet

Name of pupil ____________________ Age __________

Summary of previous assessment

Topic 1

Topic 2

Topic 3

Topic 4

Topic 5

Topic 6

Overall assessment

National Curriculum level attained [ ]

Copiable sheets

Self-assessment

1. Is my handwriting clear? **Yes** **No**
   I could make it clearer by:

___

___

2. Is my writing interesting and imaginative? **Yes** **No**
   I could make it more interesting and imaginative by:

___

___

3. Have I used different styles of writing? **Yes** **No**
   Here is a list of some of the styles I have used:

___

___

Here is a list of some of the styles I need to try or need to improve:

___

___

5. Can I write correct sentences? **Yes** **No**
   I can improve my sentences by:

___

___

6. Is my spelling usually accurate? **Yes** **No**
   I need to learn these words:

___

___

7. Can I use full stops, capital letters and question marks? **Yes** **No**
   I am making mistakes in:

___

___

8. Is my handwriting joined up and neat? **Yes** **No**
   I can make my handwriting better by:

___

___